Lion King

In the Company

Omar Octavio Albarracín Prieto

I0062322

Copyright © 2024

All rights reserved.

No part of this publication may be reproduced, distributed, or transmitted in any form or by any means, including photocopying, recording, or other electronic or mechanical methods, without the author's prior written permission, except in the case of brief quotations embodied in critical reviews and certain other non-commercial uses permitted by copyright law. For permission requests, please get in touch with the author.

Contents

Dedication

To the crown of my existence, Mariana Isabella and Gabriel Fellipe, my grandchildren.

My parents, Luis Felipe and Ana Dolores, thanks for your dedication and passion in raising me.

Acknowledgments

Thanks to my parents, Luis Felipe and Ana Dolores.

About the Author

Business administrator, specialist in management indicators and internal control of the organization, 34 years of commercial experience, 11 years as a distributor of mobile phones from Spain to Colombia, import and export between Colombia and the United States, founder of the indigenous sexy clothing brand in the USA, commercial director and general manager, team builder, currently a researcher in human behavior.

Introduction

Who is the Lion King?

Lion King Scarface

It is the story of a famous lion in Africa named Scarface. He went beyond the typical existence of a wild lion, embedding his legacy not only within the pride but also in the collective consciousness of those who knew him. Expressing his physique, social dynamics, territorial dominance, and leadership, he is known for the scar on his eye, also called Scarface, embodying the ultimate warrior by overcoming challenges and the unpredictability of the wild. His story is one of survival against all odds, parallel to human tales of teamwork, leadership, conflicts, legacy, impatience, defense, loss, powerlessness, and intolerance. Lions possess a physique that's more for strength than speed, allowing them to bring down their prey with their bodies. Scar's appearance was a canvas portraying the majesty of God's creation. As an animal, Scar was always in an endless pursuit of survival. His eyes reflected not only a beautiful amber hue but also windows that mirrored the harsh reality of life in nature. Lions possess acute senses, including adaptive vision for nocturnal hunting. Scar's transient nature of power makes him more than just a lion; he is a living narrative of daily journeys through the Masai Mara, embodying the essence of the wild with the alliance of his brothers to face conflicts. Now, human presence also influences the development of the animal's role. Human entities

1

impact the ecosystem, revealing interactions that characterize relationships between man and wild nature.

The coalitions among lions not only demonstrate territorial dominance but also showcase nuances of social structures and alliances among the strongest. Lions, as creatures, are inherently social, establishing pride and traditions to navigate the treacherous paths of nature, collectively facing challenges and seizing opportunities that punctuate their existence. Scarface embodied a leader, a warrior, and a patriarch, harmonizing power, coalition, lineage, and hunting. Together with his brothers, they defended their territory, and the social dynamics were influenced by various factors such as competition, resource availability, and the perpetual threat of survival.

Scarface was born in 2007 and passed away in 2021, adored by the community and serving as an inspiration for all animal lovers. He attained legendary status among the members of the Masai Mara Natural Reserve in Kenya, Africa. Dominating an area of 400 kilometers alongside his three brothers, Morani, Sikio, and Hunter, they formed a coalition known as the "Four Musketeers." They ruled and triumphed over everything in their path, engaging in bloody battles with hyenas and other pride leaders. Scarface, whose name symbolizes strength and resistance, was akin to the villain Scar in the movie "The Lion King." He reigned as the absolute king of the Masai Mara, leading a life filled with fights and nightly hunts. He sacrificed everything for his family, leaving behind an incomparable legacy. Like all lions, he was expelled from his pride upon reaching adulthood. In their independence, Scarface and his three brothers embarked on a journey to conquer territories throughout the Masai Mara. It was November 2010, a great adventure where the only law was to either die or become king. In 2011, they began the quest for a territory to rule, defeating leaders of other prides and expanding their influence. They added new lionesses to their group to increase their descendants, continuing their journey of conquest.

His enormous mane and appearance embellish the Masai Mara. He was the kindest and most tolerant lion with his cubs, playing with them a lot and being very permissive. Many times, he took care of them when the lionesses went hunting, even letting his cubs play with his large, dark, and fluffy mane. He allowed them to eat before him. Family was the most important thing for Scarface. Together with his brothers, they conquered around seven territories, paying the price through countless fights that left wounds on their bodies. One by one, his brothers—first Hunter, who disappeared in 2019, and later, his brother Sikio—succumbed. Scarface had to live with a hind leg injury that prevented him from hunting as in his prime. Eventually, Morani abandoned him, and Scarface became a legend of the Masai. At 13 years old, too old for a lion, he stood, caring for his prides and cubs. The king was unique, with immense power and a great personality. Thanks to this, he remained at the pinnacle of leadership for a long time, becoming the most beloved and famous lion in the world. However, age takes its toll on all living beings.

The average lifespan of a lion is 10 to 13 years, and having surpassed that age, Scarface was no ordinary lion. It means he came into the world to make history. Scarface lived to be 14 years old. Younger males noticed his weaknesses due to old age, and entered his territory, but the respect this magnificent animal conveyed was so great that they dared not touch him. Scarface understood that new leaders come, and cycles in the life of a king are fulfilled. On his own, he left the territory, not feeling in the best condition to face and fight. Finally, he abandoned his territory, understanding that he had to leave such responsibility to new leaders. On June 11, 2021, Scarface distanced himself from everything. There was nothing around him; everything was written. The KING was going to die that day, and so it happened. One of the living legends of Africa teaches us how to live and face the difficulties of wildlife and how difficult it is to reach the top, which cannot be achieved without a team where those who accompany him are the priority. His crew is his family; they are everything to him, and they must be cared for and protected. He died of natural causes, and his legacy will spread throughout Africa and the universe. He is considered the most photographed lion in the world, and you can find him on Facebook as SCARFACE.

The LION KING OF THE JUNGLE is our character in this conversation, and I have taken him as a symbol of inspiration from the animal kingdom that serves as a guide for humans in their family, business, community, or church environments—wherever you decide to apply its principles. The leadership represented by the LION serves as guidance for both decision-makers and each member of the team. I will refer to the leader as the LION KING IN THE COMPANY in this metaphorical sense, addressing men and women who hold such roles and responsibilities in any field. Those who follow them will be their missionaries. Teamwork is the backbone of this study, without neglecting all the components needed for its functionality.

I intend to agree with you on some concepts in an easy, light, simple, understandable, and adaptable way using basic language – not authoritative, not all-knowing, and certainly not dictatorial. This should serve us all for growth. Essentially, I'll use some inclusive comparisons of the lion's personality to human life from the standpoint of reasonableness and coherence in our actions.

The Lion King provides many teachings to human beings. From a biblical perspective, it symbolizes royalty and the takeover of lands and other kingdoms by force. From the perspective of being an animal, it has the ability to memorize, create its own tools, practice cooperation, work in teams, and protect family and territory. It is a majestic, beautiful living being, a true creation that God loves and cares for. Lions are expressive and affectionate but also vulnerable to injuries and diseases like any other living being. Despite being clever, they can be outsmarted by prey using intelligent tactics to evade them. Young lions can be easy prey for hyenas and other carnivores. Lions are the most threatened animals by humans, who hunt them and invade their habitats. The leadership represented by the Lion King of the Jungle, in comparison to the rest of the animal community, serves as a model for humans to encapsulate many values and actions, contributing to improving their personal and professional lives. The lion serves as a reference as a leader for humans.

We must know and explore a bit more about the LION KING OF THE JUNGLE to associate some characteristics and ways of living daily as a leading member of the pack that can help humans improve their productive environment. It belongs to the family of felines, and the most well-known species include the lion, tiger, leopard, and jaguar. The Lion King of the Jungle has a great sense of teamwork, both for the defense of the family and for hunting. Each member plays a specific role, a level of responsibility for the survival of the pack. They are capable of working cooperatively within their community and acting more autonomously in decisive moments to safeguard the integrity of the entire team. Lions mark their territory through scent deposits, requiring a keen sense of smell to protect their vital area for survival. They hunt at night or at dusk, and they may attack in a packs from various directions, surrounding their prey to minimize the chances of escape.

Communication among them is through a variety of behaviors and expressive movements that are highly developed. They engage in peaceful tactile actions such as licking each other and rubbing their heads, which is a greeting behavior. Roaring is another form of communication. Lions form groups into prides, establishing a hierarchical social structure with a dominant male. Their social body relies on individual roles, and they are the only feline animals that live in packs, making them the chosen archetype in this study.

Family units can include up to three males, a dozen females, and their offspring. All lionesses in a pride are usually related, and the young females typically stay with the group as they grow and age. Lions are social animals that live in close-knit units where females care for and even nurse the cubs of others. Males also expressively and warmly embrace their offspring.

The lion king of the jungle can reach a top speed of 80 km/h and has a powerful strength of 340 kg. According to the researcher and lion expert Craig Parker, he mentions that the main cause of death among lions in an undisturbed environment is other lions. One of the characteristics highlighted by Parker in the African lion, among the different classes of lions, is that it is ingenious, cantankerous, patient, proud, pragmatic, seemingly indestructible, beautiful to behold, and always in continuous danger.

Lions hunt in groups, and for larger prey, they use a basic strategy in the hunting process. In this approach, one of the lions detects the prey while other lions look in the same direction. Another lion hides and doesn't reveal itself until it reaches the prey. They surround it, trap it, and kill it by tearing at the hindquarters and biting the neck. This showcases the incredible teamwork of the lions of the jungle.

Lions are among the few felids that live in prides. Lionesses, the female lions, are responsible for hunting to feed the family group. The pride typically consists of six lionesses, their cubs, and two or three resident males who lead the pride.

It's good to know that part of the history of The Lion King, the most emblematic in the jungle, unfolds in Africa and Asia. Within their pride, there is a hierarchy, duties, responsibilities, rules of coexistence, and an internal communication system (chemical contact or acoustic roars among them to convey needs). There is also respect within the family, and it's not allowed for a young male to court a female from the same pride, as he would be expelled by the dominant male.

It's a species on the verge of extinction; the reproductive capacity of a male lion to impregnate a female is quite low. They must attempt mating for about four days on average, roughly twice an hour, to achieve fertilization. The gestation period lasts around three months and 15 days, resulting in the birth of two to six lion cubs. At birth, they are blind and deaf, weighing between 1 and 2 kg. Their eyes open around 15 days after birth, and they are cared for in a safe place for up to eight weeks. The mother or a surrogate mother feeds them until they reach the age of 7 to 10 months. They are protected by their entire pride until they reach the age of two when they are ready for independence.

The lion is one of the laziest animals in nature, resting up to 20 hours a day. However, in contrast to this lifestyle, it can switch to active more at any moment, driven by motivations such as hunger, thirst, hunting, reproduction, and defense of its territory. As a mammal, it belongs to the carnivore group, and its high activity at night makes it the best time for hunting. Lionesses take charge of bringing food home and are protective and vigilant, not allowing new members into the group.

Their reproduction is also composed of a harem, which, in zoology, is the habit of some species in which the male has more than one sexual partner. The lionesses are polyestrous, meaning they can go into heat at any time of the year. The male can copulate up to 3,000 times for each cub to achieve fertilization. Within prides, males often fight and compete for dominance within the group to mate with all the females. They are also constantly alert to external dangers, such as the appearance of other lions seeking to dominate their group. In fact, those who take control of pride do so after defeating the previous leaders, often leading to their demise.

There are nomadic lions, individuals who were expelled from their pride upon reaching adulthood. They may live in pairs, usually males, and some form coalitions with individuals of their own blood, such as brothers or cousins, to expand their territory's dominance and conquer other prides.

The animal kingdom respects the lion for its mindset. It hunts at night, walks without fear, is the master of its own destiny, always seeks to win, commands respect for its surroundings. It's not the largest, not the most intelligent, not the fastest, but it has courage and gallantry. It maximizes everything it does, completes what it starts, never ready to give up, fights to the death, sacrifices its life for a purpose, is always prepared, gives everything it has, shares, and relies on others.

If you want to achieve your dreams, you need to internalize, believe, harness the strength within you, seize power, give everything, don't stop, don't be afraid of the daily challenges in your life, work for your team, keep trying, keep testing strategies and methods; you will succeed.

Lions only hunt for two hours a day with a high degree of concentration. It's better that no one gets in their way. Keep fighting, keep going. The only guarantee is failure, so keep pushing. Never surrender; exhibit courage and readiness to confront challenges. Don't doubt your ability; it could cost you your life. Lions never give up because they are the kings of the jungle. They cannot show any sign of weakness. They don't make excuses; they execute, they act, and they are willing to die with dignity, with the mindset of a lion.

Believe in yourself; prey doesn't stand still waiting to be devoured. Prey runs, jumps, and defends itself. Don't wait too long; take the initiative and do whatever it takes to survive. Never stop fighting; empower yourself to be better every day. Achieve your short and long-term goals; don't get distracted from your purpose.

For the lion king of the jungle, the environment and role-play a crucial role in activating instinct. The animal responds to stimuli based on immediate needs, and these actions are encoded in its

DNA. This ensures that all generations of the same species exhibit similar behaviors. The specific function of animal instinct is to have a pre-determined adaptive response. Unlike humans, the lion king of the jungle doesn't have to go through years of learning to meet its basic needs.

This study will explore the behaviors of a lion, embarking on a mental adventure to delve into the personality of the most emblematic animal in nature, THE LION KING OF THE JUNGLE. For centuries, it has been a symbol of strength, courage, and leadership in the animal kingdom. As humans with a high capacity for discernment and natural intelligence, we can observe how we encapsulate and use it as a general objective for this study: to learn about leadership, influence attitudes in the daily lives of people, and contribute to the overall growth of the group. We will intertwine concepts such as concentration (deep work), focus, determination, and teamwork dynamics, evaluate performance with strategic planning variables, and explore how technology, specifically artificial intelligence, influences new ways of life today.

Chapter 1: The Lion King Becomes a Leader

In the Disney movie "The Lion King," Mufasa does not see his leadership role as an opportunity to wield power but rather as a profound responsibility to nurture, motivate, and inspire others.

Definition of a leader:

Leadership can be defined as the influence that a person exerts over the other members of the team. This level of influence will be significant enough for people to achieve the goals and objectives framed within a vision where the purposes aim to reach.

Leo Mindset:

For our adaptation, we could encapsulate many qualities of the LION KING OF THE JUNGLE that contribute to the leadership in our daily lives, sharing with families, communities, holding companies, small businesses, family enterprises, associations, neighborhood community boards, buildings, universities, student movements, political movements, corporations, government systems—everything inclusive of teamwork.

According to Daniel Goleman, in a business context, emotional intelligence can be more beneficial for management goals than talent, skill, or intellect.

A high intelligence quotient (IQ) can only predict 20% of the determining factors of success, while the remaining 80% depends on other variables, largely emotional intelligence.

Classification of leadership types according to Daniel Goleman

Visionary: This type of leader has a clear long-term vision and guides employees in the same direction. These leaders tend to focus on the future horizon, inspiring others to dream big and work towards the organization's vision. They have a unique ability to see the big picture and encourage their team to work collaboratively towards a common mission. Visionary leaders can instill a sense of purpose and meaning in their team's work. However, at the same time, visionary leaders can be very demanding, which may lead to disillusionment among their followers.

Coaching: The goal of this leadership style is employee development. The leader acts as a mentor, helping employees turn their weaknesses into strengths through support and understanding. They give challenging tasks to their employees and are willing to accept failure since the primary objective is personal development. This leadership style works best when employees are aware of their weaknesses and are motivated to improve performance.

Affiliative: These leaders focus on building relationships with employees, creating good harmony and a positive work environment. This model is important where individual contributions are highly valued and necessary for the business objective. In certain situations, establishing an emotional bond with employees is crucial as it helps build a sense of community. In environments with a lot of conflict, this technique can work positively by addressing personal issues and establishing trust within the company. However, a potential drawback is that the manager may avoid necessary decisions if they fear these decisions might upset team members. This can lead to prioritizing harmony over productivity, potentially reducing performance standards and hindering overall team progress.

Democratic: This leadership style is based on the idea that employees within an organization can participate in decision-making, with an equitable distribution of power among team members. Individual opinions are considered when making any decision, involving numerous meetings. It is often used when teams are multidisciplinary, requiring the combination of different skills to advance a project. However, it becomes inefficient if team members lack information on the points under discussion, as disagreements can lead to a standstill, halting the organization's progress. Therefore, it may not be applicable for rapidly evolving companies.

Pacesetting: The role of the pacesetter is to set a direction and ensure that it is maintained—do what I do, and please don't lag behind. This style is generally used by individuals who like to feel like protagonists, often when the leader is an expert in the field and the followers have less experience. This type of lion king exerts constant pressure on employees to excel, scrutinizing every mistake and dismissing those with low performance. It is advisable not to use this style for extended periods; it is better to use it in moderation and preferably switch to another leadership style when appropriate.

Coercive: This is referred to as the military approach, focusing on giving precise instructions to be followed to the letter, without employees questioning or providing input on those orders. It is recommended for specific conditions that require rapid results. Dominant leaders are free to make decisions, seize fortuitous opportunities, and take any necessary measures to achieve short-term results. This style is less likely to generate high morale among employees and may result in uncontrollable turnover.

The leader is born or made:

Some leaders are born, others are made. In the current context of football, we can observe the Argentine Lionel Messi, a high-performance athlete, who is born with special talents. He possesses multiple cognitive abilities combined with planning, coordination, sequencing, and anticipation of movements. Skills such as reading opponents, great game skills—Messi is a natural leader on the field, dedicated to his work, with the profound goal of scoring goals and leading his team to victory.

Another player in football who is born and made is the African player Sadio Mané, a philanthropist and a great natural leader in reducing inequality and lack of communication in rural areas of Senegal. He is not only a great player on the field but also recognized as "the humblest player in the world."

For him, victory is not just for the team with the best players; victories belong to the players with the best team.

From another perspective, in monarchies, leaders inherit thrones. These leaders are born into a legacy of leadership. This phenomenon also occurs in companies where descendants continue the corporate legacy, sometimes with success and at other times not. The truth is that whether a leader is born or made involves training, education, academia, empiricism, and research. Individuals can spend their lives in this process and succeed. It should be understood as a continuous learning process. Despite having innate talents, common factors include strength, passion, education, and a great inspiring spirit, much like the lion king of the jungle.

The perspectives that leaders are born, not made, have become a confusing appreciation over time, akin to a myth that hinders individual growth and teamwork. This belief can impede the development of others and, consequently, the team. According to psychological studies, leaders are born with 30% of their abilities, while the remaining 70% must be developed in individuals.

Peter F. Drucker asserted, "Leaders are born, but so few that the rest must be trained."

So, don't worry; you are a standard human being born with the same natural attributes of human creation. You, too, are a potential leader. Dare to shine.

Don't seek to lead, but to make a difference.

In the Lion King, the first step is to think about the people. Work on helping them find and pursue what they are passionate about.

Empower them to take ownership of their work. Reflect on the following topics: What type of action as a leader had the most significant impact on your team? What kind of actions do you need to perform more frequently to help your team? Also, consider what type of actions you need to eliminate because they had a negative impact on your team. What challenges do you, as a leader developing people, need to confront? What do you need to learn? What resistances do you have to improve your leadership style? What would be the first steps to overcome those resistances? What is your plan to lead better this year?

Building Leaders in Organizations

Based on the understanding that 70% is leadership training, it is essential to have an appropriate organizational culture. Work on motivating and developing the team, communicate effectively, demonstrate emotional intelligence, possess problem-solving skills, respect others, prioritize personal development, promote strategic thinking, encourage critical thinking, delegate with confidence, acknowledge mistakes with humility knowing they are part of the journey, provide opportunities for professional development, foster creativity, self-expression, and recognize that introverted individuals or those who rarely express opinions in teams often have great ideas. Learn to listen and develop communication channels, encourage active participation from everyone, and prepare them to withstand changes.

Train the talents that can lead the future of the organization. Invest in digital software solutions with information systems that enable development in the technological field and the performance of teams, which are changing rapidly in the present.

According to Tom Peters, "Leaders don't create more followers; they create more leaders."

All team members now understand that it is a multidimensional, multidisciplinary project based on individual competencies, where everyone serves as a guide in one way or another. It is crucial to comprehend the necessity of utilizing each member's talent for the team's benefit.

If your team is not achieving its proposed goals, consider options such as changing or introducing key members with different competencies who can contribute synergistically to address what is lacking and prevent stagnation.

John C. Maxwell, in the Law of the Lid, refers to stagnation. Do not all want to say yes? There are people who simply do not want to. Should not all say yes? People have their own goals and agendas; they may not be interested in the team's purpose. Can not all say yes? Perhaps they are not able to keep up with the pace of the other team members, or the expectations simply do not fulfill them.

What type of lion king do you consider yourself to be – a stick (coercive) or a carrot (affiliative)?

The stick and carrot theory asserts that if you want to get a donkey to move, you need to dangle a carrot in front of its nose and strike its back with a stick. This motivation theory has been adopted in the business realm and refers to the application of rewards and punishments to achieve goals. A carrot approach incentivizes good work with rewards, while a stick approach uses punishment to drive people toward their goals.

Andrzej Blikle, in his book "Quality Doctrine," talks about the stick and the carrot, arguing:

Punishment doesn't work: When we threaten people, we undermine their dignity. It's difficult to expect cooperation from someone we've just threatened or frightened, and if they cooperate, it will likely be driven by fear. When the stick disappears, so does all motivation to act; within the heart, there will be a desire for revenge and a sense of injustice.

Awards don't work either: When we reward someone to act, the motivation is external, and if it's external, the situation takes an unpleasant turn because it has characteristics that are not in line, such as the need for escalating rewards to achieve the same results. So, they have to reward them more and more to get their motivation. Another negative characteristic is transactionality; as soon as a person starts viewing the reward as payment, they might feel entitled - "If I do what I want, I deserve to be rewarded; if it's inconvenient,

I won't do it, and I won't receive that payment." This relationship creates friction between the expected result and a person who doesn't desire the reward.

Removing the carrot: When they take away the carrot they had promised you, it transforms the carrot into a stick. Blikle combines the carrot with the stick; any reward can be used as a punishment, and vice versa, any punishment can be used as a reward or turned into a carrot. Looking more deeply, there is no difference between a punishment and a reward; both generate the same result—they are equally demotivating and ineffective for changing attitudes in teamwork.

Traditional methods, such as the carrot versus stick approach, are no longer as effective and can even be counterproductive. It could be worked on how employees or team members understand the importance, impact, and relevance of their work in a fundamental way to motivate them. When everyone understands that their work matters and has an impact not only within the team but also beyond it, the result is satisfaction in individuals. In this context, motivation grows exponentially.

Tools to Support The Lion King in Decision-Making.

Let's explore the tools that a leader can use to make more accurate decisions and minimize errors. In this case, we will rely on stakeholders and core competencies.

Stakeholder:

"Interest groups or stakeholders both inside and outside the company" is important for the Lion King (leader) to know all the groups that exert interests inside and outside the organization for better decision-making. This theory was developed in 1984 by Edward Freeman, according to him, the theory of stakeholders considers that organizations are composed of a set of actors whom he calls interest groups.

To conceptualize stakeholders, it includes any person, entity, corporation, or company that has a certain influence or interest in the situation of a business. This interest can come from both the internal and external environments. To view it as a management tool, it would be beneficial to first reference and rationalize a general framework of what the company system is, understanding its functionalities both internally and externally. This can help create a list of stakeholders and, in the same way, use a matrix to have information at hand in order of priorities. This aids the Lion King leader in making highly assertive decisions, aiming to minimize mistakes. It is crucial to remember that such responsibility influences the team positively or negatively, and this decision-making tool should be adaptive according to the size of the project, organization, scenario, and its organic structure.

There have been extensions over time due to technological fluctuations, new competitive postures, and changing situations in markets, such as globalization. This leads to the entrance of new interest groups, changes in the importance of existing ones, and the emergence of others. Internal stakeholders include teamwork and the integration of new technological factors as contributions to teamwork. New external stakeholders for the company could be communities, environmental pollution, climate change, technology, robotics, humanoids, water scarcity, demographic growth, among others.

Stakeholders from within the company can be classified into 4 groups:

1. **Executive Stakeholders:** They experience direct effects based on the company's performance. They are interested in achieving the objectives they have set. They contribute knowledge, management dedication, and commitment, influencing the company through the control they exert over it as they are responsible for managing and directing.

2. **Shareholder Stakeholders or Shareholders:** (They are the owners of the company) They are concerned about the dividends distributed by the company and the prices of the shares since they can sell them at a higher price, generating profits. They contribute capital and the risk of investment, as success is not guaranteed. They influence the general shareholders' meeting held once a year, where new administrators are appointed or existing ones are ratified. New investment projects, budgets for income and expenses

for the following fiscal years, financial analyses, and statutory reforms are approved during this meeting.

3. **Worker Stakeholders:** They are the main ambassadors of a company and a brand, and one of the social actors that generates the highest level of trust. They are concerned about the company's performance because they want to maintain their jobs and increase their salary in the future. They contribute their workforce to the company with commitment, impacting the company's reputation. Fair working conditions must be guaranteed to prevent, for example, a decrease in productivity or a strike that paralyzes the company.

4. **Teamwork Stakeholders:** Teamwork is one of the most representative competitive advantages that a company has today. Their particular interest lies in encouraging people to develop their social skills, facilitating the achievement of common goals, increasing motivation, stimulating creativity, providing job security, well-being, and productivity, and fostering synergy. Their most significant influence is contributing to the overall growth of the organization or project. The entire team should receive credit, not just individual members. The lion king leader has the responsibility to keep them motivated; otherwise, the performance of individuals may decrease, leading to discontent, dispersion, and delays in expected results.

Stakeholders from Outside the Company:

These are individuals or groups who do not work directly with the company but are somehow affected by the company's actions and results. These external stakeholders exert influence from outside the company, and their impact is often beyond the company's control. However, it is essential to be aware of them as they interact with the organization.

1. **Customer Stakeholders:** Their concern revolves around the quality, price, and social responsibility carried out by the company. Customers are considered a vital part of the company since, without them, there would be no profits and, consequently, no business. It is crucial to listen to customers for research and the development of products and services tailored to their needs. They hold significant influence over the company because if they stop buying, the company could face significant challenges or even cease to exist.

2. **Supplier Stakeholders:** Suppliers are interested in the company continuing to operate so that they can sell their goods and services. They provide inputs or raw materials to the company, which they intend to sell in the future. Their influence lies in their ability to cease supplying these materials. From this perspective, it is recommended to have multiple suppliers to mitigate risks associated with dependence on a single source.

3. **Local Community Stakeholders:** Local communities are concerned about the company's policies, pollution, water contamination, the environment, and air quality that may affect their surroundings. They support the company through cultural contributions, social infrastructure, and communication. They can have a negative influence on the company through public campaigns, leading to a decline in revenue, decreased employee trust, and loss of confidence from customers who purchase the products.

4. **Government Policy Stakeholders:** Government stakeholders are interested in the company's prosperity, growth, and long-term sustainability to generate employment and tax revenue. The funds collected by the government are redistributed in bureaucracy, education, and healthcare. They contribute to the company through infrastructure, bridges, road networks, legal frameworks, and tax policies. They can influence the project or company by adjusting tariff rates and making changes to the legal and regulatory framework.

5. **Technology Stakeholders:** Technology stakeholders are influenced by the rapid growth of technology, which leads to structural changes in new and existing business models. Human beings may be replaced in their jobs by technological advancements. The contribution of technology lies in the use of scientific knowledge for practical applications. It is

expected to expedite and maximize production at lower costs. However, its influence can turn negative if it devalues the human element as a fundamental part of the production process.

Stakeholder Matrix:

To develop the matrix, it is important to identify two main groups of stakeholders based on their functionality and importance, which we will call primary and secondary. In the primary group, we create a quadrant where they are organized by their level of influence, as they are essential for the operability of the project or company due to their direct involvement. The stakeholders in this group include:

Primary Stakeholders	
Shareholders	Executives
Team members	Customers

Secondary stakeholders do not have a direct link with the project or company, but they are affected by its activities. This category is quite broad, but we can highlight the following:

Secondary Stakeholders	
Artificial intelligence	Climate change
Supplier system	Government

This list is very general and may or may not align with the needs of the company, which is why it's important to analyze them one by one. To do that, you need to create a chart with four quadrants based on the level of interest and influence on the company. This chart is called a Stakeholder Matrix.

Stakeholder Matrix	
High Influence and Low Interest	High Influence and High Interest (focus efforts and full attention)
Low Influence and Low Interest (minimal attention)	Low Influence and High Interest

Core Competencies:

The core competencies versus business capabilities is another factor in the decision-making process of the lion king (leader), as it allows them to understand the strengths that define a project or organization. Explain the thesis presented in 1990 by C.K. Prahalad and Gary Hamel in their article published as "The Core Competence of the Corporation," which refers to the various skills and abilities that are absolutely necessary to perform a specific role.

They presented the following analogy: "Think of a diversified company like a tree. The trunk represents the main product, the smaller branches are the business units, the leaves are the end products, and the core competencies are the roots that nourish and stabilize the entire tree."

Let's review an example that can help build a concept that contributes to your team:

Example: Let's consider a sales team for intangible services or products. What would be their core competency? It is formed by a sales department, which would be the main trunk. The Commercial Advisors would be each individual as a business unit, and the product being marketed would be the final service received by the customer. The core competency versus business capability in this scenario would be customer service.

When we talk about companies offering both products and services, it is understood that there are similar items in the market. The significant difference lies in how we can distinguish ourselves in the customer's perception, especially when dealing with essentially the same commercial bloc. The lion king must acquire knowledge about commercial skills to determine where to focus and what resources can be used most effectively to differentiate our offer from that of our competitors. In our example, the focus is on customer service as the core competency.

This characterization is achieved when the entire team aligns with this attitude. The face-to-face interaction that the commercial advisor manages should embody a stance of significant contribution, support, and trust towards the end consumer. This involves focusing on problem resolution, handling complaints, providing technical support, and considering the entire set of practices and interactions throughout the sales cycle, including pre-sales, sales, and post-sales.

Ensuring that the consumer's needs and expectations are fully met, with the essence of delighting the customer, is crucial. A satisfied customer will undoubtedly spread the company's name among their friends, ultimately boosting sales.

When we talk about companies offering products and services, it is understood that there are similar items in the market. The significant difference lies in how we can distinguish ourselves in the customer's perception, especially when dealing with essentially the same commercial bloc. The lion king must acquire knowledge about commercial skills to determine where to focus and what resources can be used most effectively to differentiate our offer from that of our competitors. In our example, the focus is on customer service as the core competency. This characterization is achieved when the entire team aligns with this attitude. The face-to-face interaction that the commercial advisor manages should embody a stance of significant contribution, support, and trust towards the end consumer. This involves focusing on problem resolution, handling complaints, providing technical support, and considering the entire set of practices and interactions throughout the sales cycle, including pre-sales, sales, and post-sales.

Ensuring that the consumer's needs and expectations are fully met, with the essence of delighting the customer, is crucial. A satisfied customer will undoubtedly spread the company's name among their friends, ultimately boosting sales.

According to the authors, they define core competency as communication, engagement, and a profound commitment to working across organizational boundaries for long-term growth. An organization should identify its core competencies and then invest in them, focusing resources on building and maintaining those skills. Prahalad and Hamel wrote that a core competency can be identified by three characteristics:

1. Because it provides potential access to a wide variety of markets.
2. They make a significant contribution to the perceived benefits of the final product for the customer.
3. It should be difficult for competitors to imitate.

The authors explain that an organization should externalize or divest in areas outside its core competencies, freeing up more resources to reinvest in fundamental capabilities. To help maintain the identified core competencies, a company should use strategic subdivisions to prioritize focus. The lion king could review its environment for competencies such as customer service, responsiveness in deliveries, product pricing, culture, strategic alliances, product presentation, and technological systems. Once reviewed, these competencies will provide the foundation from which the company, team, or project can grow, seizing new opportunities to deliver value to the customer. When you achieve this differentiation, it will not be easily replicable by new or existing competitors.

Nowadays, due to the same diversification, new components, models, and ways of working, the term core competency is applied to the strengths that individuals possess, particularly because they support that relationship with their positions in the workplace or professions. Team leaders must identify a worker's competencies as specific skills that contribute to enhancing teamwork.

MettaLeadership:

According to Roberto Mourey, a coach of High-Performance Leaders and founder of the MettaLiderazgo Institute, he proposes a leadership approach that involves moving away from giving orders and controlling, distancing itself from a lifestyle that seeks to threaten and question individuals. In this approach, people don't have any other option but to follow the leader.

MettaLeadership proposes going beyond, shifting from directing to influencing. It involves moving away from giving orders in search of a style focused on inspiring, persuading, convincing, and moving the team in the right direction. It advocates for leading one person at a time, recognizing each individual's uniqueness and acknowledging the great power within each person, understanding that everyone is different and has their own interests. If you, as the "lion king" of the company, want to inspire, persuade, convince, and move, you have to connect directly with the human being, considering that behind everything is a person, each with a different perspective. Mourey emphasizes recognizing and respecting diverse thoughts, acknowledging that a team is a moral person with its own identity as a whole.

Mourey states that a team should be 4x4, meaning it can advance independently in any terrain. Front-wheel drive occurs when an individual wants, can, and knows what they want to achieve, initiating the process because they have the knowledge and resources to do so. Rear-wheel drive is when the rest of the team says, "we want and can." When both parts agree, we have a 4x4 team.

The Culture: Your main enemy or your competitive advantage.

"Your culture is the character of your organization."

Culture is the temperament with which members collectively face adversity and emerge strengthened. It is the great self-esteem and will of each member, combined with the strength of conviction to move forward despite difficulties. The significant responsibility of a MettaLeader lion is first to define the culture needed to achieve the set goals. Working on the character of individuals can yield better results when incentivized. Secondly, designing and building it every day is crucial. Culture is the legacy that the MettaLeader leaves to the organization, team, or project. They may leave, but the culture remains. This invisible competitive culture is the power that transforms team members from behaving like victims, complaining about circumstances, and blaming others for not achieving the desired results.

The Lion King, creator of the greatest connectivity among human beings 'JESUS.'

Jesus of Nazareth informs his closest followers, his disciples, about the announcement of his death. His team gathers to discuss who could be the first when Jesus dies on the cross, sparking a debate and controversy among them in the quest for who is the greatest. Jesus tells them that the first should be the last and the servant of all. Being the greatest is not a privilege but an act of service to others.

It requires thoughtful interpretations and analysis of what Jesus Christ institutionalizes regarding leadership as a model of service and humility. A leader is not only the one who knows the most, has the most power, gives the most orders, or desires to be served and revered. Jesus says, "The last among you shall be the servant of all." In this structure, the leader is the one who serves the most, is the least visible, and ensures that others progress. Such a leader is characterized by a love for serving others, allowing others to shine, and stepping aside to let everyone grow and develop.

A leader must carefully attend to their personal life to set an example to follow. In the corporate world, it doesn't work this way;

the leader often seeks to separate personal and professional life. In the church, the leader must take care of their personal life and be a reflection or likeness of the character of God, demonstrating through actions and as an entity an example for missionaries and society in general.

Requirements or roles that a servant lion king must fulfill:

Visionary Role

Jesus is the person about whom the most has been written in the history of humanity, according to Flavius Josephus, 66 to 73 years after Christ, in his work 'Antiquities of the Jews.' In his testimony, Flavius describes them as follows:

"During this time, Jesus appeared, a wise man, if indeed one should call him a man, for he was a doer of astonishing miracles and a teacher for those who joyfully receive the truth. He attracted many Jews and many Gentiles and was also the Messiah. When Pilate, at the suggestion of the leading men among us, had condemned him to the cross, those who had first loved him did not forsake him. For he appeared to them alive again on the third day, as the holy prophets had foretold about him."

Jesus, as a visionary, focuses on the big picture: "Thy kingdom come, Thy will be done on earth as it is in heaven." Jesus' vision was never to establish a well-ordered institution like a corporation, entity, or company. Instead, he builds his church based on a community of believers who will continue his transcendent work and spread his message of love and salvation throughout all times.

Complementary Role

Serving is divine, pious, and eternal, meaning that you are following a divine pattern. God reveals Himself to humanity as a Trinity—Father, Son, and Holy Spirit. Jesus, being the Son of God made man, transcends humanity, influencing society throughout history as a leader with two natures—human and divine. Jesus, as a man, increases his knowledge, meaning he learns today what he did not know yesterday. Biblically, this is growing in wisdom and grace, a process of spiritual development. Although people initially saw him as a man, even his own community found it difficult to see him as clearly the Messiah, the Son of God. Despite John the Baptist recognizing him, people had doubts. Despite the miracles he performed, Jesus asked his disciples, "Who do people say I am? What about you, who do you say I am?" What we know about Jesus today will define our destiny. Therefore, Jesus clearly expressed his identity not only to his team, the apostles, but also through allegories, parables, and evangelization, saying, "I am the bread of life," or in other words, the nourishment of your soul. Many did not understand the message, and some intended to stone him. They could have killed him earlier, but everything had to happen according to the Father's plan, God. Jesus' complementary role as a servant is that he did not come to save angels; he came to save sinners. That's why he identified with us; he had to be one of us to solve the problem and save humanity. Bringing him where humanity should be according to God's design, not as expressed in many facets of artificial intelligence.

Chapter 2: A Focused and Concentrated Lion King

The lion king, Scarface, aptly named for his habitat, must be concentrated and focused for the day-to-day survival and protection of his pride.

Human beings are a complex system of emotions and moods. If these elements are moved within the unconscious, it can lead to actions that one may not even measure. Concentration is achieved to the extent that it is cultivated; what you think repeatedly is what truly grows in your mind.

Among Benjamin Franklin's civic virtues, there is one he called "DILIGENCE," which involves cutting unnecessary actions and focusing on what you want to achieve by eliminating what is identified as unnecessary—distractions, habits, customs, and negative influences from others.

Ludwig van Beethoven focused and concentrated his work on music, aiming to evoke emotions in people through his nine symphonies, capable of "uncovering the soul to see what lies within."

For the Lion King in the business world, it is crucial to focus on the objective, regardless of the effort required to achieve it. Many lose their focus due to a lack of total commitment. There is much work to be done, numerous efforts and tasks to overcome according to the scheduled goals in time. These goals should be clear, achievable, and measurable. If you are focused and achieve a short-term goal, design a new one. If it doesn't work, redesign and retry—don't give up. Concentrate on your strengths, design action plans, avoid procrastination, identify what doesn't serve you, and discard it. Don't insist on what you've tried and hasn't yielded optimal results. If something doesn't work, examine where the error originated, develop turning points to resume. List them, analyze them, and set them in motion again. You must be capable of achieving it; support yourself with different methodologies, reinforcing gradually and repeatedly. Work with like-minded people; by joining forces, the path can become clearer.

If you want to improve your concentration, you should know that everyone can increase it. If you find yourself in a class, meeting, or workplace and realize that you got lost at some point and have no idea what was being talked about or done, then you need to enhance your concentration to effectively focus and center yourself. If you feel like giving up on an activity or task that you chose to start, let's go over some tips to help improve your attention. You should be in good physical and mental shape; intense concentration for longer periods makes us more productive, improving results in our daily lives. On the other hand, it allows us to spend less time on less important tasks. Understand that productivity can depend on three factors: time, attention, and the energy you have. It is important to train your focus capacity. The result of work produced is equal to the time used multiplied by the intensity of attention while performing that task. So, you can spend a lot of time on a task, but if your attention is deficient, the results will be too.

In today's world, our attention is under constant threat from mobile phones, WhatsApp, notifications, chat, SMS, social media addiction, and thousands of sales applications. People today struggle to sustain their maximum attention on a chosen topic for more than 15 minutes in a row. Therefore, we must learn to manage our brains, which are wired to pay attention to pleasurable things, threatening situations, and new stimuli.

The key to reclaiming our attention is to use it consciously, turning off autopilot and identifying what is most significant. It's easy to concentrate when the interest or survival is at stake. When training your concentration, do it with the most relevant tasks, avoid procrastination, eliminate sources of distraction such as the phone (put it in another place or on airplane mode), isolate music, TV, loud external noises, and train the rhythms of your attention and current capacity.

Take a watch or stopwatch, and time the activity you have chosen to focus on without getting distracted. Start with the watch in hand, consecutively. Once you notice your mind wanting to wander elsewhere, note the time you remained focused. Your goal is to increase this time each time. If you endure for 4 minutes the first time you try, note it. Take breaks between intermediate points and repeat the exercise several times to improve your own record. The objective is to understand and identify how often your brain wants to get distracted. Once we understand our cognitive state and concentration, we can utilize other tools discussed in this chapter.

Deep Work (Trabajo Profundo):

In utilizing the Deep Work technique, we will draw from Cal Newport's book to define some techniques that can be adapted to our daily lives and work.

Deep Work, according to Cal Newport, is a set of professional activities carried out in a state of concentration devoid of distractions, such that cognitive abilities reach their maximum limit. This effort creates value, enhances skills, and is not easily replicable.

We will review the book "Deep Work" ("Céntrate"). I will share a summarized version to make the knowledge about deep work more accessible. The book has two main purposes. The first part aims to convince you to work deeply in both your professional and personal life. The second part addresses how to do it in a world full of distractions.

There are two approaches to work: shallow work, which is the opposite of deep work. Shallow work consists of tasks that are not a cognitive challenge, can be performed in a distracted environment, do not create significant value, and are easy to replicate. In the current world, there are numerous distractions like Facebook, Instagram, YouTube, phone calls, paperwork, meetings, etc. Newport argues that there is a tendency toward shallow work, but he emphasizes that those who resist this trend and commit to deep work are the ones who will stand out in the market. Working deeply is crucial today for two reasons:

1. We live in a world that is changing too fast. People who have the ability to learn quickly will succeed. In other words, there is a bright future for those who learn to master deep work.

2. The interconnection of people who require high-value work will triumph rapidly. This means that products or services of high quality will prevail, while those creating mediocre things will be easily replaceable.

Working deeply is valuable. Many activities cannot be executed in the same way with deep work, it doesn't apply to everyone, but it does for the majority. Deep work is scarce; we often confuse busyness with productivity. We engage in what is easier and might appear busy, like watching videos or scrolling through our phones, but if your job is about producing, you are not doing it optimally. Working deeply makes sense not only for professional or career success but also for various benefits in your personal life. This is based on three main arguments: neurological, psychological, and philosophical. Where you focus will yield results. It's better to work deeply, intensely, for four hours a day and spend the remaining time on less critical activities, like meditation or spending time with family. Working deeply is a key component of the success of prominent entrepreneurs, such as Bill Gates, who isolates himself for two or three weeks each year in a cabin to draw important conclusions for his company.

Let's quickly look at the second part of the book, which is the rules:

Rule Number 1: Work Deeply. We all have a limited amount of willpower each day, and the faster we deplete it, the less we'll have. The key to success is to create routines, environments, and habits that help you work deeply, so you don't have to exert too much willpower in that regard. For example, the Harry Potter series author, J.K. Rowling, faced numerous interruptions while trying to finish her latest book at home. To counter this, she decided to rent an extravagant hotel room and locked herself in until she completed her writing.

There are four philosophies that we can adopt. The first one is the monastic philosophy, which involves scheduling deep work by isolating oneself. For example, going to a cabin or taking a season to work on what is most important to you. The advantage is that it seeks to maximize concentration and focus by distancing oneself from all factors that lead to shallow work. Those who use this method are individuals with a well-defined goal or purpose, and their success depends on doing that task exceptionally well. Cal Newport acknowledges that this method is for very few people.

The second philosophy is the bimodal deep work philosophy, which involves retreating to deep work for periods or seasons. In other words, you engage in monastic work but with alternating periods for other activities. For example, you might spend a semester doing deep work and then return to your normal life.

The third philosophy is to have deep work routines, suitable for people who cannot disappear from their daily lives. They choose a daily time period, for example, working from 9 am to 1 pm, developing well-defined work habits.

The fourth philosophy is the journalistic one, which consists of dedicating your free time to what you have to do without distractions. This method works for people with many capabilities, confidence, and previous achievements who know they can accomplish it. We can extract some tips that can help us:

First tip is to ritualize, create routines and habits instead of procrastinating and wasting energy. For example, be clear on which day, at what time, for how long, and where you will dedicate yourself to deep work, study, writing, or work. It should be evident that it is a part of your life.

A second tip is to make exceptional gestures, such as changing your environment, to send signals to your brain that this is important. Create something exceptional and different to help focus.

The third tip is not to work alone. The book discusses the concept of open offices, revealing a management tool to **work as a team**, collaborate, and make public commitments that hold you accountable for what you said. Working as a team is beneficial, as different thought sources can help solve problems more effectively, providing better solutions.

The fourth tip is about discipline. According to Cal Newport, the first thing is to focus on what is truly important. Sometimes, we want to do many things at once, but spreading oneself too thin can lead to less impact. Focus on one or two goals that are truly important to you. For overly ambitious goals, break them down into smaller, achievable steps. Concentrate on these steps to reach the larger goal. Another discipline is measuring actions with basic result indicators – either you achieved it or not. Predictive indicators will help you consistently achieve good results. Continuously measure your progress with indicators like A, B, C (priority map) to stay on track. For example, if you want to learn a foreign language, a predictive indicator could be how much vocabulary you've learned, the hours available, etc. These indicators set a goal, such as learning 10 verbs daily, watching movies, listening to audios, reading the newspaper. If you meet these goals, you'll achieve the result of speaking another language. Another discipline is to maintain a results board, visually displaying your daily, weekly, and monthly progress. Wishing you much success in your endeavors!

Fifth tip is embrace the lazy. Our brains have a limit to cognitive abilities, and sometimes disconnecting, taking breaks, and changing topics are beneficial for the brain to recharge energy. Open the doors to boredom; the ability to concentrate is a skill, like a muscle that needs exercising. Cal Newport argues that we have a low tolerance for keeping our attention focused. Even when we want to concentrate, we may find it challenging, so we need to make certain reservations about connectivity with social networks. Cal suggests that this ability to concentrate should be a habit, a lifestyle, like athletes who take care of their bodies with good nutrition and sleep. Don't take breaks in distraction but in concentration. Ideally, schedule your breaks and tasks with less time than you think you'll need, so you have free time. Meditate productively and professionally, plan an outdoor walk to think about solving a problem, practice memorization techniques, and distance yourself from social networks designed to be addicting. For deep work, dedication, willpower, and acquiring intense concentration are essential to reach the limit of your capabilities. Delegate social networks; Cal suggests finding a middle ground where you assess how much they really contribute. Eliminate the superficial. Even the most experienced individuals struggle to maintain a high level of concentration and focus for more than four hours. Schedule uninterrupted work periods during the day, while the rest of the day can be utilized for less intense tasks, events, conferences, emails, networks, and spending time with family. In other words, organize superficial work in a block of hours during the day so that deep work is not interrupted.

Cal Newport extols Bill Gates' capacity for deep work. Bill learned about the existence of Altair, the world's first personal computer, featured on the cover of Popular Electronics. Gates immediately saw an opportunity to design software for the machine. Walter Isaacson explains, in an article published in 2013 in the

Harvard Gazette, how Gates worked with such intensity and for such extended periods during that two-month period that he often collapsed in front of the keyboard while writing code. He would then sleep for one or two hours and resume work where he left off. Isaacson defines this as a feat of concentration and a serial obsession.

Newport argues that deep work is a pragmatic acknowledgment that the ability to concentrate is a skill that allows us to accomplish valuable things. In other words, deep work is essential not because distraction is bad, but because it allowed Bill Gates to create a billion-dollar industry in less than six months.

Meditation:

The late Mexican scientist Dr. Jacobo Grinberg, who disappeared in 1994 without a trace until today, proposed the synergetic theory. He stated that meditation in a single location by two individuals triggered a connection of thoughts between them.

Meditation can induce a state of deep relaxation and a calm mind. During meditation, you focus your attention and eliminate the flow of confusing thoughts that may be filling your mind and causing stress. This process can result in an enhancement of physical and emotional well-being. Meditation is a mental training that is far from clearing the mind. On the contrary, while meditating, you are engaging in something much more practical: developing qualities such as mindfulness, compassion, optimism, and managing challenges like stress and obsessive thoughts. It stops mental wandering and builds more connections between different parts of the brain. In Jacobo Grinberg's self-referential meditation book, he states that meditating is the path through which he can recover his original unity with the universe without losing his presence in the human world. It is a door through which he can reclaim his cosmic essence as many times as he wants and, once strengthened, continue his path here and now.

The objective of this meditation is observation or self-observation of one's totality. It involves integrating all elements of experience to reach consciousness of unity, combining the individual and universal aspects, somewhat connected to mindfulness. Essentially, it seeks the cultivation of concentration. Grinberg states that it is necessary to harmonize some elements. One component is the breath; if the mind becomes distracted, return to the breath. Another element of observation is the body, traversing all sensations and unifying them. Next, you familiarize yourself with the mental phenomena of observation. You don't observe thoughts but their flow; you don't observe images, memories, or emotions individually. The goal is simultaneous observation of the entire experience—observing everything at once as a whole.

When you can achieve simultaneous observation of all elements, something strange happens. You reach a threshold where things begin to be different. In other words, you connect with yourself, managing to bring all these elements into consciousness to enhance the synergy (a neologism that combines synthesis and energy) of your neuronal field. This integration forms a more potent algorithm that prevents your attention from shifting from one place to another.

Mindfulness Meditation: Mindfulness meditation involves being fully present in the moment, observing thoughts without attachment, and cultivating awareness. It is widely practiced to reduce stress, improve concentration, and enhance emotional well-being.

According to Buddhists, it is the practice of transforming the mind to reach its maximum potential, as the world's primordial nature is consciousness, not matter. This transformation surpasses the ordinary limits that a secular materialistic society ascribes to reality.

Tibetan monks have a technique that involves focusing on their breathing, counting each inhalation and exhalation. They start by taking in air through the nose and exhaling through the mouth, repeating this slowly up to three times. Afterward, they continue breathing only through the nose at a normal pace, not too slow nor too fast. According to the monks, this meditation exercise helps quantify the focus of the mind. They also frequently use the **single-point** meditation, which entails concentrating all attention on a single objective or task. It is ideal for calming the mind and focusing consciousness. The chosen target for the exercise can be external or internal, but one must focus solely on that point, staring fixedly at a single spot like a small object, a black dot, or the flame of a candle.

Neurological effects of meditation

The effects that meditation has on the human brain have been known for years and are the subject of ongoing research. New studies are released almost every week, revealing more benefits. The positive neurological effects are extensive, ranging from changes in gray matter volume to improvements in the interconnection between brain areas. Some benefits include:

1. **Reduces activity in ego-related brain centers:** Mindfulness meditation has been shown to reduce activity in the brain network responsible for self-referential thoughts. This helps individuals gain control over wandering thoughts by forming neural connections through meditation practices.

2. **Slows down brain aging:** Long-term meditation practitioners have been found to have better-preserved brains compared to non-meditators. Studies indicate that individuals with over 20 years of meditation experience exhibit more gray matter volume, suggesting a more youthful brain. Gray matter is crucial for higher cognitive functions such as memory, language, abstract thinking, and consciousness.

3. **Aids in controlling depression and anxiety:** Mindfulness meditation has demonstrated its ability to reduce symptoms of anxiety and depression. Regular practice helps individuals cultivate mental habits that contribute to emotional well-being.

4. **Improves memory and concentration:** One of the notable benefits of meditation is its positive impact on attention, memory, and concentration. Even after a few weeks of meditation, individuals may begin to notice improvements in cognitive functions.

5. **Assists in overcoming addictions:** Mindfulness meditation has been compared with conventional smoking cessation programs, showing that individuals practicing meditation are more likely to quit smoking. This suggests its potential in aiding recovery from various addictions, including alcohol, drugs, and overeating.

6. **Stress management:** An 8-week mindfulness meditation course has been shown to reduce the size of the amygdala, the brain region associated with fear and stress responses. This reduction contributes to improved stress management as the prefrontal cortex, linked to concentration and decision-making, increases in size.

7. **Decreases perception of pain:** Advanced meditation practitioners often report experiencing less bodily pain. Meditation may alter the perception of pain and increase pain tolerance.

8. **Enhances social skills:** Regular meditation has been associated with improved social relationships, suggesting that individuals who meditate regularly may have increased responsiveness to others' feelings and enhanced empathy.

9. **Reduces feelings of loneliness:** Meditation as a mental exercise has been found to decrease feelings of loneliness. This reduction in loneliness is linked to a significant decrease in the risk of mortality, suicide, and depression.

10. **Promotes longevity:** Regular meditation practice has been shown to reduce telomeres, essential parts of human cells that influence the aging process. By reducing stress and promoting patience, meditation may contribute to a longer and healthier life.

11. **Controls heart rate:** Eight months of meditation practice has been associated with a decrease in heart rate and respiratory rate. This indicates the potential cardiovascular benefits of sustained meditation.

12. **Reduces the risk of Alzheimer's and premature death:** Thirty minutes of daily meditation has been linked to a reduced risk of premature death, Alzheimer's disease, heart disease, and depression.

Mindfulness (Conciencia plena):

Mindfulness increases the well-being of those who practice it, aiming to train the mind to focus attention and concentration by redirecting thoughts. It is considered a life philosophy acquired through the practice of meditation, an ancient technique that has been in use for over 2500 years with the goal of enhancing the quality of life. Mindfulness seeks to concentrate attention on the present moment, fostering full awareness of what is happening here and now. It involves focusing on oneself and the surroundings, letting go of noise and distractions, serving as an excellent tool for self-control. The objective is to achieve a deep state of consciousness, aiming to prevent the mind from passing judgments on sensations, thoughts, and feelings. Mindfulness encourages dedicating time to experiencing the environment with all senses – touch, hearing, sight, smell, and taste. This relationship significantly enhances focus, performance improvement, conflict resolution, and overcoming negative thoughts. Focusing on the present moment can positively impact health and well-being. Mindfulness-based treatments have shown reductions in anxiety, depression, blood pressure, and improvements in sleep. The good news is that anyone, regardless of age, religion, gender, language, or profession, can practice this meditation technique. A recommended time for mindfulness practice is often in the morning, before becoming deeply immersed in daily activities. Adopting a comfortable posture, one observes what happens in the mind, body, and environment. This initial observation may reveal a "monkey mind," a restless mind jumping from one thought to another. Through mindfulness, attention is exercised like a muscle. Practicing for a few minutes each day and gradually increasing to at least 30 minutes is advised. Perseverance is crucial, and finding a quiet time during the day, such as in the morning, before bedtime, or after lunch, is essential. Choosing a tranquil environment without noise and distractions, maintaining a comfortable posture, and focusing on the breath are key components. With practice, the technique improves, and over time, thoughts and emotions arise freely, requiring a neutral stance – neither judging them as good nor bad but perceiving and observing them in an impersonal manner.

The practice gives me the opportunity to be in this space and moment, reacting in a less compulsive and impulsive manner, considering the conditions that arise. It means functioning less on autopilot, allowing us to make freer and more appropriate decisions in each situation.

Dopamine:

Dopamine, chemically speaking, is a catecholaminergic neurotransmitter that is crucial in the central nervous system of mammals. In other words, it is a molecule responsible for transmitting messages from neurons that produce it to other cells. Therefore, it plays a role in regulating various functions such as motor behavior, emotion, and effectiveness, as well as in neuroendocrine communication.

Dopamine helps the brain control motor functions, movements, and possibly performs other functions related to mood. An imbalance of dopamine can lead to brain dysfunction and disease. It is also known as the "happiness molecule" as it provides pleasure (a tool of Cupid to inspire love) and relaxation. Dopamine is involved in memory and learning processes because it regulates the duration of memories, determining whether specific information can be stored for a period or is immediately eliminated from our brain.

In teamwork, dopamine serves as a source of motivation in the development of daily tasks. Dopamine performs its task before we obtain any reward, meaning its true role is to encourage us to act and achieve the team's objectives. If all team members have a good level of dopamine, it controls information levels in the brain, enhances memory, attention, and learning, and also plays a role in problem-solving.

As the "Lion King" of the company, if you want to harness this tool to motivate your team, ensuring they are focused and concentrated, start by getting to know them. Understand what they like, what keeps them happy in their job, what their expectations are, what their long-term goals are, among other factors not mentioned here. These responses will determine, with more or less emphasis, motivation, effectiveness, efficiency, and daily productivity.

Dopamine is also known as the hormone of reward and satisfaction. It is stimulated through exercise, listening to music, sex, meditation, and when achieving set goals. Dopamine also motivates us to seek pleasant situations or activities while avoiding negative ones.

The amount of dopamine in the cerebral amygdala, which is the brain region related to emotions such as anger, pleasure, or fear, allows us to understand if a person is calm, insecure, or easily stressed. High levels of dopamine in the prefrontal cortex of the brain make individuals more motivated to meet demanding goals and concentrate on their work.

How to increase the dopamine levels in your team:

There are truly many elements that can increase dopamine levels in your team and with which you can play:

How to win an award or anything out of the ordinary, if the whole team manages to reach the goal at the end of the week, month, or project time, our brain rewards us with dopamine to motivate us to obtain that prize, meaning if things go well and we achieve victories. Other sources of motivation to consider include leaving work an hour early, a day off, a surprise gift, sharing successful experiences with the rest of the team, and undergoing training that teaches us and helps us reach our goals. Therefore, dopamine is an ally for all team members in achieving objectives because it provides pleasure in obtaining rewards and recognitions. Work on it like the Lion King, and you will see excellent results in your team.

Pomodoro Technique:

This time management method was developed by Francesco Cirillo, a computer engineer who created the technique in 1980. The technique uses a timer to divide the time dedicated to a task. "Pomodoro" means tomato in Italian. It involves alternating "pomodoros" (sessions of concentrated work) with short and frequent breaks to promote sustained concentration and prevent mental fatigue. It is a time management method that suggests working in intervals of 25 minutes without interruption or distractions and adding 5-minute breaks. The goal is to set tasks and improve productivity.

Remember that tasks requiring more than 5 pomodoros should be divided into smaller, manageable tasks. Small tasks (like responding to emails) can be grouped into a single pomodoro. If your workday is 8 hours, make sure not to set more than sixteen pomodoros in a day.

During the 5-minute break, you can engage in any other activity you like, such as checking emails, using social media, getting up from the desk, walking, taking a breath, or stretching your legs. The aim is to disconnect and stay ready for the next pomodoro, avoiding burnout. Every four pomodoros, it is recommended to take longer breaks of 15 to 20 minutes.

Yagé Technique of the Indigenous People:

This technique does not have a scientific basis, and I want to share it as informational. It is used from an ancestral perspective, facilitated and performed by indigenous people in some countries. However, there is no precise foundation to endorse its use. It is simply known to exist and is employed by many common individuals, including students, professionals, academics, politicians, housewives, and some tourists who seek to have such experiences.

Yagé is a large climbing shrub that produces woody stems that can reach up to 30 meters in length. Extracts from this shrub have become a traditional remedy used for thousands of years in the Amazon rainforest and the Andean region in countries such as Brazil, Colombia, Ecuador, Peru, and some regions of Bolivia and

Venezuela. In Colombia, the yagé brew consists of a mixture, boiled or cooked, of the Banisteriopsis Caapi vine with a plant with a high concentration of Dimethyltryptamine (DMT) like Diplopterys cabrerana (chagropanga).

It is a kind of purgative or indigenous drink that has a comprehensive effect on the physical, mental, and spiritual aspects. It is important to include it here due to its purposes that are directly related to the topic discussed in this chapter, which is concentration and focus. Just as there are other techniques scientifically endorsed by psychologists, therapists, psychiatrists, doctors, there are also ancestral practices like yagé that have some cleansing effects on physiological, psychological, and spiritual impurities. If there is such a relationship between a healthy mind and a healthy body, from that perspective, one could think that concentration and focus might be easier for people who engage in these practices.

The ritual is led by a shaman or "taita." Shamanism is part of the Ainu indigenous religion and the Shinto religion in Japan. Since the early Middle Ages, Shintoism has been influenced and syncretized with Buddhism and other elements of the continental culture of East Eurasia.

The shaman is a highly trained individual within the indigenous community who travels to different areas of these countries where they are invited to perform rituals. They can control time, prophesy, interpret dreams, engage in astral projection, voluntarily separate the spirit from the body, enter other worlds, and gain access to subtle matters, the soul, spirit, and life energy.

According to research conducted by the Colombian anthropologist Juan Camilo Perdomo Marín, an independent researcher in a bulletin of anthropology from the University of Antioquia, Colombia, in his article "Bebiendo los cabellos de DIOS: buscando aproximaciones teórico-metodológicas a las ceremonias de yagé en Colombia" (Drinking the hairs of GOD: seeking theoretical-methodological approaches to yagé ceremonies in Colombia), he presents important data to share in this discussion. Perdomo explains that yagé ceremonies are emerging intercultural scenarios that have spread throughout Colombia in the last two decades, mainly through healers belonging to indigenous communities in the foothills of the Amazon. These healers have built and consolidated extensive networks of urban and rural patients within the national territory, and ceremonies are also conducted outside the country in retreat centers or periodic rituals in the United States and Europe. These rituals tend to begin with a brief discursive introduction by the yagé healers about the effects of the brew and the cosmology in which the ritual is embedded. They then offer a brief prayer to the yagé and distribute it to the audience. Within minutes of consuming this drink, the physical purging effects (vomiting and diarrhea) manifest, accompanied by profound synesthetic states (sensory experiences occurring simultaneously). In the midst of the trance, the shamans (indigenous wise individuals) ensure the protection of all attendees by singing ceremonial chants and spreading incense smoke. As a ritual closure, there is a search for spiritual cleansings. The quest for new spiritual and medicinal experiences has fueled the contemporary demand and receptivity of these rituals among a general audience and academics. People tend to participate in these ceremonies because they seek visions in the trance (known as "pintas"), which they interpret as a means of revealing inner knowledge. On the other hand, they seek prevention or healing from diseases, mental problems, and psychological traumas that they consider are not effectively treated by scientific medicine. They do not expect any substantial change in the world but rather a subjective transformation of the individual itself. The goal is to establish a lost bodily balance and gain knowledge about the social world and personal life. Through the visions of the trance, patients would learn ritual chants (which they recite cyclically like mantras) and images would emerge that indicate their physical and mental health states.

It is important to explore other perspectives on how humans, in search of new alternatives for achieving inner cleansing, engage in the initial premise of preparing their brains, minds, and hemispheres. This involves intertwining and aligning states of consciousness, unconsciousness, and the subconscious in the quest for balance. This pursuit aims to develop the capacity for concentration and focus on individual goals across various existential realms, whether personal, familial, academic, corporate, project-related, teamwork, or tasks requiring a high level of concentration.

A foreigner who visits Colombia, Africa, and other countries to experience indigenous and traditional medicine, such as the yagé or ayahuasca brew, shared his first encounter. The YouTuber, named Lethal Crysis, narrates that during his initial experience, he had visions involving people he cared about, close individuals like his parents. These visions allowed him to connect with them on a personal level, perceiving aspects of their lives that were not apparent in his normal existence. Lethal Crysis explains that subsequent intakes resulted in different sensations. He describes the brew as a means of connecting with oneself, a profoundly personal experience that alters emotions and consciousness with one's own truth. The brew has the capacity to transform negative energies into positive ones, filling individuals with authentic love and contributing to the cleansing and balance of body, mind (concentration and focus), and spirit. Additionally, it fosters personal growth in individuals.

Chapter 3: A Determined Lion King

In human society, we admire the courage, strength, and power of Scarface, the scarred face warrior, the true lion king of Samay who ruled over 7 prides and conquered territories with great determination. Alongside his team known as the Four Musketeers.

The lion king of the jungle earns his title not by being the biggest, smartest, or fastest, but by his mindset and determination to achieve what he sets out to do.

If you want to be a lion king with determination in your team, work hard every day, earn the respect of each member, showcase your competence and perseverance in the workplace. Inspire others to follow you, radiate energy, make it a part of your emotions, vibrate, and give your best in everything you do. Fight, strive, regardless of the circumstances. Prepare yourself, listen to them, protect them, love them as your own family.

The lion king of the jungle does not tremble at the laughter of hyenas; do not let your guard down as long as you breathe. You are responsible for your successes and failures, no one else. Adapt, make changes when necessary; you decide whether to live like a sheep or fight like a lion. A lion's mindset is determined to achieve its goals, facing whatever comes without hesitation, with decisiveness. Be intuitive, become an expert at climbing walls or leaping over them. Be persistent, become the soul of the pride, the soul of your team.

Definition of determination:

From the perspective of internal connection, it is when I intertwine with my being. I can get to know myself, identify my weaknesses and strengths, and at the same time, I am capable of questioning what I want to become, what I want to be. What metamorphosis do I want to achieve, how will I do it, in what time? What am I willing to sacrifice? What price am I willing to pay? What attachments am I willing to release through my willpower? In the journey, there are stumbling blocks, difficulties, and moments of wanting to give up. Determination is an internal force that nourishes me, provides tools, involves decisions. It is not idealism; determination is to act, to have strength, fierceness to achieve my goals, always seeking to be happy. Surely, we must accumulate good habits every day to achieve excellence. If we can sustain excellence, we will become ethical individuals in society.

Determination is the force that enables you to conquer dreams or face difficult situations. It is the decision you make to continue no matter what, helping you feel fulfilled in what you do. However, you must assume responsibility for such a decision; you cannot unload it onto someone else. You realize the power of this decision when you have clear goals and pursue them with your utmost energy and attitude.

Kobe Bryant, the American basketball player, played with the mindset of "today is the day." He knew that this day was the only one he controlled, ensuring to put his heart and soul into every ounce of effort.

Nayib Armando Bukele Ortez, the current President of the Republic of El Salvador, leading the smallest country in the Americas, began his presidency in one of the world's most insecure nations. He decided to overturn the history of his people, plagued by social issues, by taking the determination to confront gangs and imprison them, aiming to provide what a society needs the most: freedom and security.

In the Declaration of Independence, Thomas Jefferson determines the following for human beings:

We hold these truths to be self-evident, that all men are created equal, that they are endowed by their Creator with certain unalienable Rights, that among these are Life, Liberty, and the pursuit of Happiness.

Arturo Calle is one of the most recognized and beloved brands among the Colombian public, serving as an example of determination for new entrepreneurs worldwide. The growth of his organization is rooted in savings, humility, and avoiding debt, while investing in human capital. He integrates his team as missionaries, considering them an extension of his family within the company.

For the Lion King from a business perspective, determination involves finding answers, never giving up, and never settling for current results. It is crucial for companies to avoid failure and closure due to a lack of perseverance. The renowned psychologist Angela Lee Duckworth, who has dedicated part of her life to researching the causes of success, makes a clear reference to the power of determination. She asserts that beyond the talent a person may possess, determination is the key as it encompasses passion and perseverance. It is holding onto your future while living in the present, producing rather than just working, to make that future a reality. "Live life as if it were a marathon, not a sprint," she says.

Life story of the most determined man in technology, Steve Jobs, the founder of Apple:

He never completed his university studies. Jobs was given up for adoption by his biological mother, who initially wanted a girl. His mother hesitated to sign the adoption papers when she learned that his prospective adoptive parents were not professionals, but eventually did so. At the age of 17, he enrolled in an expensive university that his parents could barely afford. However, after six months of questioning the value of university education and realizing it was depleting his parents' life savings, he decided to drop out. At that moment, he stopped attending classes that seemed unimportant to him and focused only on those he deemed relevant. Life wasn't easy; he slept on his friends' dorm room floors, sold soda cans for food, and walked 7 miles across the city for a good meal each week.

As he continued his journey, serendipitous events occurred, and one notable example was taking a calligraphy class. Although he initially saw no practical application for it, this knowledge proved invaluable when, ten years later, he designed the first Macintosh computer with beautiful typography. He emphasized the importance of connecting the dots in life, stating that it's challenging to see forward but clear when looking back.

Jobs, along with his friend Steve Wozniak, started Apple in his parents' garage at the age of 20. Over ten years, Apple grew from a garage company to a $2 billion company with over 4,000 employees. However, at the age of 30, after creating the Macintosh computer, he was fired from the company he had founded. This was a devastating blow, and Jobs spent several months feeling lost and disappointed.

Undeterred, he started over and founded a new company called NeXT and another one called Pixar. He also found his life partner, Laurene, who created the first computer-animated film, "Toy Story," which became one of the most successful studios globally. Interestingly, Apple later acquired NeXT, and Jobs returned, bringing the technology developed at NeXT to spark Apple's revival.

While his departure from Apple was a bitter pill, Jobs believed it was the best thing that happened to him. The following years became one of the most creative stages of his life. Reflecting on his journey, Jobs shared his belief that loving what you do is crucial, and work should fill a significant part of life. He emphasized the importance of persevering in finding what you love and not settling until you do.

Jobs shared a profound reflection: "If you live each day as if it were your last, someday you'll most certainly be right." He adopted the habit of asking himself every morning, "If today were the last day of my life, would I want to do what I am about to do today?" If the answer was "no" for several days in a row, he knew he needed to make a change.

Jobs reminded his audience that time is limited, urging them not to waste it living someone else's life. He encouraged people to have the courage to follow their hearts and stay hungry and foolish. Steve Jobs passed away on October 5, 2011, in Palo Alto, California, United States. His last words were, "OH WOW, OH WOW, OH WOW."

Tips to develop the determination of a lion king in his team:

1. Establish that what you are fighting and working for is what you truly desire, with internal strength from the deepest depths of your being.

2. When faced with an obstacle that hinders your path, repeat, persist, and resist until you overcome it.

3. Act with confidence, as if you have already achieved what you desire; do it with certainty.

4. Remember that success may be within your reach, just before the next challenge you take on.

5. Make radical decisions in what you want to achieve. Cling to your dreams rooted in your heart with the firm determination to triumph.

Jim Rohn, an American entrepreneur and leadership coach, once mentioned that the best definition of determination came from a high school girl in California. He loved talking to young people because they come up with wonderful things. The girl said, "Mr. Rohn, I think I have the definition. I think determination is promising yourself that you will not give up." Rohn expressed that it was the best definition he had ever heard. There's no need to promise anything to others, nothing to the world. You just have to make the promise to yourself.

People should keep trying until they find answers. How many books will you read until you have good health and avoid cardiovascular problems? As many as necessary, right? Wouldn't you read books on financial independence until you are financially independent? Wouldn't you read leadership books until you become a leader? Wouldn't you read books on power until you gain power? Wouldn't you persist in building a good team until you achieve it? If you want to be a leading figure, you must prepare until... Don't settle for less; use the word "until." Exercise enough until you are healthy. Impose disciplines on yourself until you're out of breath. When you embrace this mindset, your life will take a turn.

Jim Rohn's Contribution to Determination:

Jim Rohn provides questions that help us cultivate determination. The first question is "why?" Don't let any "why" pass without a substantial answer. When you have a powerful "why," the "how" becomes easier. Sufficient reasons propel you forward. The

67

second question is "why not?" How many skills can you develop, how much money can you share, how many people can you help, how much can you contribute to your team? Why not get involved in various ventures, make more sales, generate new prospects this month, achieve promotions in your company, improve as a parent, sibling, or child in your family? Why not make new friends, explore all your possibilities and values in life, and enhance your relationship with God? Live an extraordinary life—go wherever you want, because why not?

Why not you? If other people can, why not you? If you can't read, can't change, if others can set disciplines and save themselves from failure, why not you? Can't wake up earlier, why not you? Can't work harder, does your blood have less ambition than mine? Success stories in the United States are about this - a woman like Mary Kathlyn Wagner, an entrepreneur and founder of Mary Kay Cosmetics, started by selling books in a patriarchal era where women were socially discriminated against and managed to become the best businesswoman of the 20th century. She left a legacy where women could achieve success, transform their lives, help others, and be recognized equally in the United States. That's what the stories of the American Dream are about. If one can do it, why not you?

JIM provides the example of his friend Mark Hughes, the founder of Herbalife Nutrition Foundation (HNF). Mark faced challenges in his early life, including drug use. However, he managed to escape this lifestyle and became deeply interested in helping others overcome drug addiction. Even from a young age, he started fundraising. Mark became one of the best teenagers, winning various awards. Today, he is a great social philanthropist, dedicating a significant portion of his fortune to helping young people overcome drug addiction.

One of Mark's clients was Ronald Reagan, who later became the President of the United States. Mark did not meet his father until the age of 20, and their initial relationship was not positive. Unfortunately, they did not see each other for nine years. Eventually, they decided to become good friends and succeeded. Mark had a challenging upbringing - a judge had to decide with whom he would live when he was a child, and it was not the best-case scenario.

At the age of 18, Mark's mother died of an overdose. Mark did not attend college; he only went to school until the ninth grade and then dropped out. After his mother's death, Mark realized there had to be a way to lose weight without becoming addicted to drugs. He decided to explore a nutritional and safe method, studying nutrition for 2-3 years and making a groundbreaking discovery - herbs. Fascinated by them, he even traveled to China as a young man.

Mark formulated a product called Herbalife, and his grandmother was his first customer. She lost some weight, felt good, and spread the word. Herbalife started with Mark selling products from the trunk of his car and gradually expanded. He gained more customers, reached $1 billion in sales, and then another $1 billion.

Mark continued to expand to other countries, reaching extraordinary success. He encouraged others by saying, "Why not you?" and advised taking full responsibility, facing challenges, and seeking a way out. He urged people not to settle for less, to be inspired by stories like his, and to start from scratch, even in debt or desperation. Finally, JIM's last message was to seek the help of God.

Another example of determination is the Colombian entrepreneur and philanthropist Carlos Ardila Lülle. In the year 2000, he received the Entrepreneur of the Century award. According to Forbes magazine, he has been among the top thousand richest men in the world. He is an example of overcoming challenges, hailing from a middle-class family. "I regret nothing in this life. If one does not take risks, if one does not fight, if one does not strive, well, things cannot happen overnight."

The determination of the UN regarding water, the most important natural resource for humanity:

The second specific meeting on water in almost half a century convened by the United Nations (UN) seems extremely important when discussing determination and self-determination of emerging action. "When a winter of global discontent approaches," says the UN. This is where global leadership must intervene, especially when it involves human beings in their entirety, regardless of race, religion, beliefs, political parties, politicians, ethnicity, or continental location. A critical issue that world leaders and ordinary people must address is the fight to preserve water.

Let's focus on what happened in 2023 within the framework of the United Nations (UN) in New York, the United States. A conference was convened by the international community to assess the progress made but also the limitations and obstacles hindering the actions of the international community to ensure adequate access to the sanitation of this precious resource - water. This evaluation included considerations of the impacts of global climate change on the hydrological cycle, geopolitical competition, and the challenges of water security.

Simultaneous multifaceted crises threaten the future of humanity amid a planetary crisis due to the exploitation and fierce competition for natural resources. The devastating effects of climate change have brought the issue of water to the forefront of the international agenda. According to the UN, one in four people worldwide lacks access to safe drinking water. The world must now turn towards finding solutions to address the current water crisis, as this resource is vital for the preservation of life, economic growth, sustainable development, and poverty alleviation.

Contributions from world leaders regarding the discussed topic:

Contribution from the Government of Honduras to the UN:

In parts of the presentation by the President of the Republic of Honduras, Xiomara Castro, she stated, "With the purpose of addressing the global issue of water sustainability and sanitation for the entire population, this is a challenge that all nations of the world assume. First and foremost, it is essential to acknowledge that the problem of access and distribution of water originates from the accumulation model that governs the world – capitalism. Resolving this issue requires much more than conferences, global agreements, or relief programs. Solving the water problem is related to understanding that the issue lies in neoliberal policies and the capitalist system. Therefore, we must advocate for a structural change in the system."

She continued, "Global powers and highly industrialized countries are the main polluters in the world, while so-called developing countries are the permanent victims of the effects of pollution due to social and environmental vulnerability. It is not enough to provide cheap labor or import goods and products at high prices; we also must endure the worst consequences of climate change. Each year, our winters become more irregular, and our summers hotter. We go from seeing our cities and productive valleys flooded to suffering from drought and lack of water. We witness with great pain and concern the massive migrations of our people due to climate change and its harmful effects."

"However, our presence here today is not only to denounce the model and insist that no real change is possible unless the countries that make up the world elite renounce their opulent and destructive ways of existence. Honduras presents itself to this water conference as a worthy, sovereign, and autonomous nation that, despite its limitations, is taking actions to achieve the fulfillment of the 2030 agenda, Goal 6 on water. Honduras is willing to collaborate and join efforts with other nations and organizations to preserve the life of the planet. Nevertheless, mutual respect and recognition as equals must be a non-negotiable condition because interventionism and the imposition of any power are no longer permissible. We are the architects of our destiny, and we will build it through **self-determination**."

António Manuel de Oliveira Guterres (secretary-General of the United Nations)

Emphasized the critical role of water in sustaining humanity, ecosystems, and biodiversity. He highlighted the challenges of overconsumption, unsustainable usage, and the impact of climate change, stating that the world is facing an urgent water crisis. Guterres outlined four key areas for accelerating efforts to address the current water situation. Firstly, he stressed the need to close the water management gap, urging governments to develop plans ensuring equitable access to water while preserving this precious resource. He called for collaborative efforts among countries working across borders to manage water resources. Secondly, Guterres emphasized the importance of investing in sanitation and water-related initiatives. He urged all nations to apply the Water Convention, SDG incentives, and proposed reforms in the global financial architecture to increase investments. Financial institutions were urged to find creative ways to expand funding, with multilateral development banks urged to increase support for water and sanitation projects in desperate nations. In the third area, Guterres underscored the necessity of upgrading water infrastructure, calling for investments in resilient distribution systems and disaster-resistant purification plants. He highlighted the need for innovative recycling methods, intelligent food systems that protect climate and biodiversity, and reduced methane emissions. The fourth key area focused on combating climate change, with Guterres emphasizing that climate action and a sustainable water future are intertwined. He called for intensified efforts to limit global warming, proposing a climate solidarity pact where major emitters increase emission reduction efforts, and wealthier countries support the transition of emerging economies. Guterres concluded by urging swift recognition of water as a driver of economic development and a human right. He emphasized the need for commitments to change the trajectory of actions for the Water Agenda to progress, stressing that it is time to acquire such commitments to ensure a sustainable water future.

Pedro Arrojo:

The UN Special Rapporteur on the Human Rights to Safe Drinking Water and Sanitation raised concerns about water entering the futures markets of Wall Street. He highlighted that considering water as a mere economic commodity, akin to oil and gold, is a misconception. Arrojo emphasized the critical distinction between water, a fundamental human right, and commodities like oil.

He expressed apprehension about the impact of water futures markets, which traditionally operate in the realm of commodities, allowing major buyers and distributors to speculate on future prices. While this mechanism may stabilize prices for large buyers and sellers, Arrojo warned about the risks associated with allowing large financial corporations or banks to enter these markets. Their substantial financial resources can influence and manipulate speculative prices, potentially leading to monopolistic control and speculative pricing that favors the financial institutions. Arrojo characterized this situation as a "casino economy," where the financial institutions tend to benefit at the expense of fair and equitable water access.

In essence, Arrojo emphasized the potential dangers of allowing water, a vital resource for human survival, to be treated as a tradable commodity within speculative financial markets, raising concerns about the impact on global water accessibility and pricing due to monopolistic speculation.

Feedback:

All human beings need to make decisions and take responsibility for the global water crisis that directly affects each of us today. The presentations offer three perspectives on the issue: one from a Latin American country, Honduras; another directly from the United Nations (UN) through its Secretary-General; and the third from the UN Special Rapporteur on the Human Rights to Safe Drinking Water and Sanitation. The common thread is the emerging global water crisis, prompting reactions from major world powers and fostering a collective awareness of the importance of this precious resource.

It is crucial to take action, defined as the decisive and firm act of making choices, involving governments, human rights advocates, and individuals alike. Starting with simple practices at home, such as saving water by minimizing shower time, closing taps while brushing teeth, fixing leaks, and using water-efficient techniques, can make a significant impact. These efforts not only save money but also contribute to preserving water sources, maintaining a healthy environment, and nurturing ecosystems.

Encouraging a culture of water conservation through education at home, in schools, and through campaigns by businesses and local governments can amplify the impact. If determination is applied to these actions, breaking the predictions of global water scarcity becomes achievable.

Benjamin Franklin, a founding father of the United States, instituted 13 civic virtues to guide good habits and conduct, including temperance, silence, order, determination, frugality, diligence, sincerity, justice, moderation, cleanliness, tranquility, chastity, and humility. Today, three new virtues are added: protecting animals, safeguarding the environment, and conserving water.

Chapter 4: The Lion King Works as a Team

Scarface, the Scarred Face, was an inspiration for all animal lovers, leading a pack of three brothers who ruled for several years as the strongest lions in the African territory—a united pride bound by brotherhood and blood, making them invincible.

Definition of Teamwork

It could be defined as the way to have influence over other people. This influence can be perceived positively or negatively.

Peter Drucker: "Each team has its own characteristics, structure, and behavior demanded from its members. Additionally, they have their own limitations, requirements, and scope."

Bill Gates: He emphasizes the importance of prioritizing the team's needs over one's own and being always honest.

John C. Maxwell: Teamwork is not just about gathering individual talent but cultivating an emotional connection that forges a powerful synergy among members.

Is it worth working in a team? Considering that people are naturally different, with diverse opinions due to factors like religion, politics, academic background, and life roles, conflicts, bosses, rules, and the tendency to delegate work to others may arise in a team. Sometimes, individuals prefer doing things on their own and achieve positive results.

Another question is, can you achieve great purposes alone? Where two people are engaged in an activity, teamwork is already in progress. Despite being interdependent, they work together for a common purpose, making a collaborative effort to achieve a goal.

In today's context, individual work has diminished, and it is crucial to integrate skills, abilities, and competencies to reach corporate goals. It becomes the lion king's task as a leader to form successful teams, look after them, and lead them to development, considering the human condition implicitly from various perspectives, fostering good synergy to unite them all.

It is a task of the Lion King, a leader in shaping these successful teams, to watch over them, guide them in their development, taking into account implicitly the human condition from various perspectives. This involves fostering good synergy to bring them all together.

Undoubtedly, the great projects and advancements of humanity cannot be accomplished alone; we have to associate, join forces, leverage strengths, competencies, aspirations, and dreams. Superheroes are just a fiction embodied in characters like Superman, entrenched in our minds as super-powered individuals capable of fighting and winning battles and wars. They do not exist as such; humans have achieved significant progress for humanity through teamwork.

Michael Jordan, the greatest basketball player of all time, said, "Talent wins games, but teamwork and intelligence win championships. I can accept failure, everyone fails at something, but I can't accept not trying."

In teamwork, idealizing is beneficial as it serves as the fuel to forge a clear vision of where to collectively go. However, it is not sufficient without taking the necessary actions. To achieve operational efficiency, human and financial resources implicit in the project planning are needed. An important aspect in team formation is identifying what can be accomplished with them, what they are capable of achieving. As the Lion King, it is crucial not to make a mistake in this selection, as the initial formation may dissolve. Humans are multifaceted and disjunctive, making an interdisciplinary team necessary for its varied competencies. Everyone should break free from external constraints, identify their roles in the work environment, focus on their assigned tasks, considering each person's individual identity. Despite diverse backgrounds in culture, religion, upbringing, and customs, team members can come from anywhere. As the Lion King, you must choose an effective team for the hunt.

Forming a team (according to Bruce Tuckman)

Getting a group of people to cooperate is not an easy task, ensuring they are prepared for potential unknown obstacles, and above all, keeping the project on track is not easy.

Bruce Tuckman (1938-2016) demonstrated in an article titled "Sequence of Development in Small Groups" that focused on the interpersonal relationships of group members and the impact these relationships had on daily tasks. He shows us through team behavior that, during its formation, all teams must go through the following stages:

1. Formation: In the "honeymoon phase," team members are getting to know the objectives and tasks, identifying opportunities and challenges they must face. All participants begin to acquaint themselves with each other, especially in expressing their individual preferences. Issues that are not usually comfortable should be discussed, and there is a risk of conflict. According to Antony Raymond, a newly formed team goes through a "honeymoon" period characterized by uncertainty, as team members are not yet clear about their assignments or the expected performance level. Raymond provides advice for navigating the formation stage.

Advice 1: Encourage open communication among team members.

When the staff meets for the first time, it's important to provide a platform for open dialogue where team members feel comfortable sharing their thoughts and opinions. Meetings and interactions can be established; the more they interact, the quicker trust is built, establishing team dynamics.

Advice 2: Establish project goals and milestones.

It is crucial to have a clear idea of the main project goal and all the milestones that must be achieved. As a leader, having a clear vision of the path before the first team meeting facilitates easier communication of objectives.

<u>Advice 3: Define roles and responsibilities for each team member.</u>

The leader's prior work comes into play here, organizing roles and responsibilities clearly, precisely, and in writing. Aligning people's competencies with their tasks is essential. The set of roles and responsibilities for each member should be clearly understood; otherwise, people might assume that certain tasks belong to others, leading to confusion.

<u>Advice 4: A great team begins with its selection.</u>

Each selector has criteria for personnel selection, framed within the organizational culture, personalities, character, capacity, adaptability, availability, knowledge, academia, experience, family background, records, skills, and abilities. All of these factors, together, can vary according to the project's needs.

2. Turbulence, Storm: "The honeymoon is over." This stage cannot be avoided; it is where different opinions are voiced, and conflicts arise, especially when defining each person's roles. Divisions within the group inevitably emerge, particularly regarding power dynamics, status, and role definition. For some, this stage is exciting, while for others, it can cause anxiety and potential dropout. Many teams get stuck in this stage, even after progressing on the ladder; returning here is essential to create solid foundations. According to Anthony Raymond, the honeymoon is over, and challenges arise that can result in a deadlock, especially when two parties disagree on the direction the group should take. Each believes their proposed solution is the best, and determining the correct path may not be easy. At this moment, the leader must step in with an executive decision. However, Raymond notes that the chosen decision often turns out to be incorrect. Accepting this responsibility is one of the greatest leadership challenges. You are responsible for your team's victories as well as their mistakes. You must make each tough decision with confidence, even when there is little reason to trust any of the options.

3. **Normalization**: In this step of the ladder, resolving conflicts strengthens group cohesion. People now know how to tolerate each other's peculiarities, each understands their responsibilities, and tasks are assigned, developing an awareness within the organized hierarchy based on everyone's competencies. Once these barriers are overcome, the team is ready to move to the next step. In this stage, energy, connectivity, and performance begin to grow again. People start engaging in conversations, including difficult ones, and feel encouraged to give and receive feedback. The internal well-being perceived by the team is also reflected externally, affecting stakeholders, leaders, and all individuals involved with the team.

4. **Performance:** Each individual performs their tasks interdependently; the project is already in progress. Different opinions provide feedback to the team, and when roles and agreements are well-defined, teams often achieve immeasurable levels of success. However, if internal or external changes occur, the team may need to return to the storming stage. In this stage, we can

observe a self-sufficient team with self-management, possessing all the resources to resolve and achieve their goals. They don't require a leader constantly instructing them on how things should be done; just by indicating, they have the capability to execute, find their own challenges, and devise mechanisms to fulfill their purpose. In this stage, energy is high, performance, effectiveness, and a sense of pride and belonging are at their peak.

5. Dissolution: The project has successfully concluded. Final closure meetings and congratulations are likely to take place. It is also important to conduct an evaluation of the mistakes made, open for discussion as preparations for the next project begin.

As a way to extend the analysis, we cannot expand this method of forming your work teams in a linear manner. The analysis becomes a bit more systemic when engaging with the current reality, where new participants are included in our teamwork.

Analysis of the Tuckman Model

The process of team formation in these five stages cannot be viewed as linear, especially when dealing with people. Individuals bring conflicts, frustrations, emotional highs and lows influenced by their daily lives. Another challenge arises when teams encounter obstacles and need to pause to discuss their direction; this can lead to a return to the storming stage. These disruptions can occur numerous times during the project's development.

Often, these eventualities in the storming stage require a reevaluation and the adoption of a fresh approach, leading the team back to the normalization stage. What happens in this fraction of time is the team adapting to the new circumstances to continue forward. As a prospective measure, the best action a leader can take to minimize this friction is to develop contingency plans for handling unforeseen events, preparing the team for any potential setbacks and preventing project delays. On the other hand, it may happen that the project is prolonged or extended over time.

Approach of the New Teams:

A team to succeed needs talent, hard work, technology, effectiveness, and efficiency. A special condition is leadership. If a team has great leadership, then it can obtain everything else it needs to achieve the goal. The leader must be a motivator, transcendent in the message to colleagues, taking them beyond the usual boundaries, improving their performance, and raising their expectations to the maximum. For these results, teamwork is essential.

If current organizations understood that teamwork is a competitive advantage, where the focus is on developing leaders at every level to be more efficient, Peter Drucker emphasizes in the knowledge society the importance that the human being should have in the organization. It should not be valued as a liability but as an asset. Having a good team implies having good results. Steve Jobs is often praised for his innovative mind, but behind the scenes, Jobs had a team of designers, programmers, engineers, and creative marketers. Often, this can cause jealousy, with the leader receiving the praise. The director of iPhone design once showed a degree of discomfort but also said the following:

If Steve were not here with us, the ideas that arise from me and my team would have been completely irrelevant. He is the one who propels us and overcomes all resistance to turn our ideas into products.

According to Peter Drucker, focusing solely on functional areas in today's organization is not enough; instead, the focus should be on knowledge-based aspects such as education, research, development, and innovation.

In creating teams, "The Lion King" in the business, it is crucial to consider the mix of components where human beings predominate in their construction and make them successful and sustainable over time. It's not worthwhile to establish teams that dissolve quickly or easily return to the previous stage, as we learned from Bruce Tuckman. Planning, organization, direction, and adequate resources directed by true leadership with clear mission and vision are essential.

Work teams are made up of people, and people are social beings, born and living as members of a community integrated into society. Individual humans would be isolated, incapable, and defenseless. Instead, individuals think and act in teams that work together, combining efforts with common goals for a clear objective to reach the maximum vision.

One of the greatest betrayals an organization of individuals can commit is attempting to form a working team or transform a group into a team through a decree. Such an approach often lacks genuine appreciation. Many times, team leaders aim to achieve cohesive results in people through this formula, but it has not yielded the best outcomes. However, numerous advancements have been made in developing teams, and among them is a key source: motivation. Recognition, a form of motivation that appeals to all human beings, stands out as one of the best approaches.

Incentives for Your Team Members

Mary Kay once said, "To be a good leader, you have to understand the value of praising people on their way to success."

People will resist if an active reward system is not established. Rewards motivate individuals, and without motivation, long-term support will diminish. The system needs to be adaptable to implement changes without resistance. In many cases, intrinsic rewards hold more value than monetary ones, with mental and spiritual rewards gaining significance in today's context. Recognition should be a team management system developed within the company to motivate people. However, it is often the least understood management method in companies due to inherent flaws. It is a tool used to motivate people, but its implementation is not always clear. It is essential to recognize that it can have negative effects when evaluating creativity. Studies show that providing incentives for tasks requiring basic creativity can hinder innovation.

In such cases, the more incentives provided, the longer it takes to solve the problem. Leaders today cannot rely on outdated carrot-and-stick techniques; they must consistently seek methods that foster self-motivation with key elements in personal development and productivity.

Today's leaders cannot rely on old carrot-and-stick techniques; they must work to find techniques that often develop self-motivation with key elements of people's development in productivity. For example, emotional salary includes additional values that contribute to human integrity in society, such as non-economic benefits that allow personal satisfaction, quality of life, social well-being, family reconciliation, physical well-being, sports activities, recreation, integration, and flexibility in work schedules.

As the Lion King, we must find ways to convince people within the organization to perform their tasks better. To achieve this, we must also define consequences for both parties, starting with the company's management. Workers also have consequences if they do not fulfill them, and all of this must be within the framework of each country's labor development and regulatory codes. The legal aspect is different; we cannot talk about punishments to impose. Surely the most relevant punishment is that these individuals are not involved in the following projects; no one likes to be sidelined and not taken into account. Everything must be related to internal regulations and local legislation. If they introduce work incentives and they are not fulfilled, there are consequences. The goal is to induce a certain behavior. The individual will act as a relational object, evaluating costs and benefits; therefore, the objective is to optimize the behavior sought by the incentive designer. In the management program, economic and non-economic recognition incentives can be developed. An incentive program can help, but first, the ailments of the staff should be determined in the empathy stage, such as helping them achieve their goals. Listening to them instead of conducting cold surveys, some objectives could be a decrease in staff turnover, rewarding greater effort, increasing productivity, increasing commitment levels, improving the work environment, and increasing emotional salary. These objectives must be achievable and stipulated within the implementation timeframe. You should develop a budget for these incentives, create a simple template or matrix, or a dynamic table with its variables. Consider income and expenses for each item; the important thing is to know the investment, costs, time savings, and return on investment.

Economic Incentives

Economic incentives are those that involve a financial or monetary contribution and can be applied to different salary components such as overtime, commissions, bonuses, etc. They are the most commonly used incentives, and their rationality and implementation often depend on the size of the company. Here is a classification of economic incentives:

1. **Natural Incentives:** These are based on human nature itself. Humans are beings driven by curiosity, and they can be motivated to do certain things to meet their basic needs.

2. **Financial Incentives:** People expect financial rewards or economic income such as salaries and commissions for their hard work.

3. **Moral Incentives:** These are incentives in which people's actions are considered right or admirable.

4. **Coercive Incentives:** These incentives emphasize negative consequences or punishments and do not succeed in motivating people internally since the activities are carried out out of fear.

Non-economic Incentives

Non-economic incentives are increasingly used by companies to motivate work teams as they offer an extra appeal to working conditions. In some cases, they are intangible but generate trust in people.

1. **Flexibility of hours:** It can be established within the project that if activities are carried out on time, special considerations regarding time could be granted. Flexibility can be managed in its analysis by determining which types of positions can be granted these awards. For fundamental positions, before considering, check if it can be covered by another person with the same or higher capacity as the person receiving the benefit. Let's put an example: a heavy

machinery operator is an important position, or a manager responsible for tool distribution. Some positions naturally find it difficult to receive these benefits to avoid inconvenience. You can manage special time by time; this means that, for accumulated time, you can give a day off, obviously paying the salary, to cover all team members equally.

2. **Recognizing achievements:** When people achieve a goal of any size, recognition is important (Dopamine). What is significant is that there is an authority, so to speak, in the same functional area or department that makes public recognition of the achievement this person has accomplished. It is important because it increases the sense of belonging in the organization. Typically, human resources make these recognitions. It is good to design recognition schemes. It could be a special format, a diploma, a plaque, or simply a format with letters and special colors of the corporate image, or allusive to something emotional for people that they can stick to the front of their desk or workspace in a visible place for them. Assimilation and valuation are different if it comes from the human resources area; it is perceived as external to the work area. It is more important for people when they get involved with those around them; it becomes more important. Recognitions have to do with the sense of belonging. A high motivation source

is that recognition comes from the group we belong to permeate more about the organizational culture. When we achieve all those sums of feelings, we are fuller, we feel self-realized, and we surely reach the highest point of Maslow's pyramid, self-fulfillment. If you manage to consolidate this scheme, it can be a great option to get better results in your team.

3. **Creating a good work environment:** When an evaluation of the work environment is done, we can detect what needs to be improved. Word of mouth is the best way to perceive what people require at that moment. There is nothing more pleasant than working in a place where you feel comfortable. This includes many things: a dignified, illuminated, fresh place, harmony of colors, comfort, good treatment, recognition from the people around you, feeling valuable to the organization. Those responsible for implementation and monitoring are everyone, including human resources, middle management, high management, and all levels of leadership.

4. **Fostering a sense of belonging:** The sense of belonging must be developed in people in such a way that they feel proud to belong to the organization. This point is directly related to the previous one. In a healthy environment, people want to spend more time in the company, where they can express themselves freely, feel that their contributions are valued, feel comfortable being themselves with transparent

communication, and be appreciated as individuals. Some companies develop strategies for their employees to feel at home and be part of it. Some of their actions are distributed among them. It is seen a lot in large companies or holding companies that are listed on the stock exchange, although also some SMEs. Other companies develop objects that carry the company's logo, such as cups, utensils, wallets, caps, shirts. They must be of very good quality to generate pleasure in putting them on or using them; this makes you proud to belong to that organization.

5. **Generating expectations for the future:** It is very good for people to know what will happen in the future with the company to feel more secure. This implies directly with their family plans. It is very good to tell you what happens and happens this year, the next, and the next to all people, especially in growth and investment plans, just like what is planned to improve for them. Sell the idea of where we want to go because we need them, and without them, we cannot achieve it. What are we doing to help them reach that prospect with us? Always act with honesty and transparency so that people in general value our actions. This expectation is important for middle, managerial, operational levels, and the community in general in the sense of perceiving what development I (personal development) can have in the company, what more achievements I can obtain, how I can

advance individually. If the work is safe, it is surely associated with my development.

6. **Choice of Days Off and Vacations:** People need to take a break, disconnect, and take a breath, precisely so that when they return, they can see things differently. It is important that people can choose those days off, and when it comes to vacations, take them at the times dictated by labor regulations. It is not advisable to have people without rest for too long; they become overwhelmed, and other implications arise. From the moment you hire people, they should know when their vacations are, and they should take them. Encourage people to take a break.

From another perspective, when developing management plans related to recognitions and economic and non-economic incentives, take into account personal, departmental, and company achievements in the schematization. We must establish activities that encompass all three incentives. Let's look at why. If we only consider personal criteria, we will get highly competitive individuals, but there is likely poor communication among them. These individuals do not talk to each other; they limit themselves to competition and selfishness. We must also establish departmental or functional objectives so that one person helps another, forming teams. But what happens if there is no communication between departments? We must establish ties or organizational criteria, integrating them as a whole, and thus, we can have a high-performance team.

Organizational Culture

It is the set of rules, customs, beliefs, and values that an organization establishes to have its own identity and positively influence its members.

Chick-fil-A Organization:

Chick-fil-A is a fast-food chain in the United States with expansion in several countries worldwide, boasting over 2,400 restaurants and over 10 billion dollars in annual sales. It is the number 1 chicken sales chain in the United States of America and is closed on Sundays. Sunday is the second busiest day of the week for fast-food restaurants, and analysts suggest that opening on Sundays could potentially increase sales by 20%. However, the founder, Mr. Truett Cathy, explained the reason for not opening on Sundays. When asked about his legacy and how he wants to be remembered when he's no longer with us, he responded, "I want to be remembered as someone who kept priorities." These priorities are the secret to Chick-fil-A's success: first, honoring God through a relationship with Jesus, teaching how to love God and people; second, prioritizing family; and third, emphasizing work.

The decision not to open on Sundays is rooted in these priorities. The business is framed by biblical principles, and Cathy's strong Christian beliefs have significantly influenced the company's culture and values. Commitment to ethical business practices and a desire to serve the community have shaped the corporate identity. The Golden Rule, treating others as you want to be treated, is part of their business model—leadership through service.

Chick-fil-A's core values include top-down control, genuine care for employees, a culture of caring, and strong values such as addressing the physical, emotional, and often spiritual needs of individuals. For employees, there are scholarship programs for those who work with the company for two years. The average working hours per person are 20 hours per week, and there are camps for children and other scholarship programs. Their corporate compass has a moral direction to thank God, meaning giving back a portion of the blessings received to others and helping the people they come into contact with. They are an inclusive culture leveraging the strengths of their diverse talent to innovate and maximize their focus on operators, team members, and customers, driven by purpose.

Some organizations attempt to delegate the responsibility of organizational culture to the human resources department. While this department is involved in personnel-related tasks, such as managing, controlling, and performing systematic activities like timely payroll, contract preparation, conflict resolution, and creating technical sheets for organizational climate, organizational culture runs deeper. It involves the character of individuals, and these characters collectively shape the organizational climate, which influences individual results and performance significantly. Organizational culture is a factor influencing both administrative and non-administrative practices and attitudes of organization members. In the context of The Lion King as a new leader, leading people and managing resources, workplace culture today relates to the balance between personal and work life, their development, sustainability, innovation, and purpose.

The majority of authors assume that recognizing values, integration rituals, organizational identity, norms, among other aspects, are fundamental for studying an organization's culture. In this study, it can be said that the organization consists of three dimensions: organizational structure, coordination systems with control, and organizational culture. All three dimensions are of paramount importance for a company's operational effectiveness.

Main Characteristics of Organizational Culture

Values and principles

Apple: Technology is most powerful when everyone can leave their mark. Our goal is to leave the planet better than we found it. We design Apple products to protect your privacy and give you control over your information. We believe in a safe, respectful, and supportive workplace for everyone.

Corporate principles and values refer to the beliefs and convictions that decisively influence the behavior of members of an organization. These principles guide and determine how the members or participants of a team or organization perceive and interpret problems to make sound decisions.

Corporate principles, being a set of beliefs and values, function as guides that inspire the life of an organization. Within an adaptive list of organizational principles, many could be enumerated in view of our missionaries, but we are talking about honesty. It is not enough to list them on informational posters; action must be taken and truly practiced. It is not about complying with corporate regulations but living them with personnel, being role models in their business role with these four protagonists: people, family, company, and community. Some corporate principles can include respect for people, ethical values, social responsibility (water, environment, waste), product quality, profitability, productivity, and humanized resources. Corporate values are aspects that make your team or company different from the rest. It is not the brand, the logo; they are deeper aspects that generate a personality that creates a competitive advantage over others.

Work environment

Also known as organizational climate, it can be defined as the set of activities, routines, and conditions that occur within a company and are directly linked to the satisfaction of workers in their work environment. The organizational climate can be clearly identified with the observation and perception of individuals regarding the quality and characteristics of organizational culture. That is, culture represents the true image of the company, while the climate reflects individuals' perceptions of it. A good favorable work environment is characterized by a productive environment that facilitates the performance of collaborators or missionaries, always promoting their well-being.

Traditions

Preserving and promoting traditions and rituals helps improve commitment, retain job performance, and enhance talent in individuals. It is a set of values, beliefs, norms, traditions, behaviors, and practices shared by members of an organization. These traditions vary according to the country and could be of religious, historical, and cultural origin. Traditions help us in work teams to connect with each other; they serve to transmit feelings, social values, and a collective memory.

Business ethics

The 10-Foot Rule is one of Walmart's secrets for customer service. Sam Walton, its founder, encouraged associates to take on this commitment: "I solemnly promise and declare that to every customer who comes within 10 feet of me, I will smile, look them in the eye, greet them, and ask if I can help them."

Business ethics is the set of values and norms that arise from the culture of the company, aiming to improve aspects such as the environment and work climate. It promotes equality and respect. Ethics is also the code (values, mission, vision, rules, prohibited behaviors, conflicts of interest) that guides individuals in individual behavior regarding what is right and wrong, not only in decision-making but also in daily conduct and routine, as Sam Walton inspires his team. If a team acts ethically, motivation and satisfaction of each member will increase, group cohesion will be generated, and the company's image will improve, all of which increase the chances of success. In teamwork, ethics helps us actively participate in the pursuit of a common goal, subordinating personal interests to the team's objectives.

Chapter 5: The Lion King evaluates his team today.

"SCAR" is strong, courageous, protects against hyena attacks, and cares for the great circle of life.

In teamwork, the Lion King in the company can develop a strategic plan to move forward with an evaluation of measurement parameters based on internal and external competencies that can develop competitive advantages, growing everyone in the purpose.

FADO Analysis

We will rely on the FADO analysis tool (Strengths, Threats, Weaknesses, Opportunities), which is a technique within strategic planning that can help the Lion King assess how his team is today, projecting into the future.

Definition of FADO

FADO is a comparative evaluation of team progress. Constantly reviewing strengths and weaknesses as internal variables, and threats and opportunities as external variables. The administrative researcher and consultant Albert Humphrey invented the SWOT analysis in the 1960s at the Stanford Research Institute. Over time, different scholars of the subject have expanded its concepts and incorporated new contexts due to changes in today's business. For this assessment, the combination of these variables does not matter as long as it is known which ones are internal and external to the team. To assimilate and yield the same results, we will use synonyms whose names connect us with other current realities in concepts. What exercises action within the team, internal: strength = resistance, weakness = fragility. What exercises action outside the team, external: threat = warning, opportunity = convenience. Leveraging the logic of the mathematical principle "commutative law," the order of factors does not alter the product, and we proceed to its analysis.

Internal Environment

Strengths = Resistance: These are situations that arise within the team or organization, and what is inside is directly controllable by the Lion King of the team. You should review what resistances your team has compared to other teams or projects within the company. We will mention some items that serve you in this identification or analysis stage to consider in the next step when creating the list for the matrix: situational leadership, punctuality, high compliance rates, conflict navigation, high-performance roles, self-organization, shared responsibility, assertive communication, emotional intelligence, trust throughout the team, technology, production capacity, adaptability, commitment, ambition, economies of scale (the more a good or product is produced, the lower the cost should be; this leads to lower unit costs compared to competitors), high-profit margins, investment in marketing, innovation and new product development, machinery, tools, financial resources, organizational culture, work environment, empowerment, emotional salary, teamwork.

Weakness = Fragility: This variable is also within the team or company, and what is inside is directly controlled by the Lion King. You should identify what failures or weaknesses your team has today. Weakness is a set of internal factors that place a team or organization at a disadvantage or disadvantage compared to its closest competitors. I will list some items that will help you in this analysis stage when you create the list for the comparative matrix. The results of these associations will help you develop the strategic plan. Some items include lack of leadership, belligerent bosses, lack of liquidity, multitasking (referring to the ability to perform several tasks at once), difficulty working in a team, individual work, high dependence on the leader, processes are ignored, lack of role awareness, few problem-solving skills, lack of proactivity, negative attitude, pessimism, lack of empathy, lack of smooth communication, low task completion rates, intolerance, reluctance, ability to change rapidly, bifurcation, procrastination, weak research and development, lack of innovation, obsolete technology, demotivated people (remember that one transmits to others; the energy of the negative grows more quickly). Some teams have incompetent leaders, which is also a weakness or fragility in the team. Dr. Robert Sutton, a professor of administrative sciences at the Stanford School of Engineering, has spent much of his life studying belligerent bosses. In 2007, he wrote a book called "The No Idiot Rule."

Anthony Raymond, in his book "Good Boss and Leader," recounts the following anecdote from Space X: "We have a strict no idiot policy. We fire people if they're idiots. We give them a little warning first, but if they keep being idiots, then they're fired."

Identification of idiot bosses or leaders:

According to Dr. Robert SUTTON, he identifies several revealing characteristics of idiot bosses or leaders. Unfortunately, when people are put in positions of power, these things happen. People tend to focus more on satisfying their own needs rather than those of those around them.

- Insult employees.
- Look at them angrily.
- Treat them as if they are invisible.
- Yell and insult them.
- Violate the personal space of others, such as getting involved in their lives.
- Are naturally sarcastic.
- Are good at threatening employees.
- Use tactics of humiliation and shame.
- Interrupt when employees express their opinions.
- Betray the team's confidences to advance their professional goals.

If you want to learn more about the topic, search online for the ARSE tests, and you can take free online tests if you wish. The test is not intended to be an academic tool; rather, it is designed to help monitor people's behavior. If you answer positively to any of the questions in the test, you may be on track to graduate as an idiot.

External Environment:

Threats=warnings: Threats are outside the team or company, not controllable by the leader. What the leader does is adapt, assume a defensive position, or simply disappear. Some of the following items will help you identify the top threats on your matrix list. In the environment, factors such as: divided areas, general company policies, social factors decided only by the leader, team members not knowing each other, cultural factors, demographic factors, ecological factors, structural changes in the organization overall, recession, market variations, macroeconomic government changes, inflation, unemployment, informality, not having certifications or licenses to trade in some countries, or their own states. Labor laws in some countries favor the employee, especially in more developed ones. For example, firing an employee is easier for them to quickly find another job. But in less developed countries, unemployment rates are higher, and workers are more protected, making labor laws more stringent. For example, firing an employee involves paying severance, and this dichotomy directly affects the team, project, or company in general. If we talk about companies selling non-essential products, a warning is that competing is more difficult, especially with substitute products in the current market due to globalization, which leads to low prices. We must face this threat by removing products from our catalog that are not highly profitable, that have completed a cycle, or that simply contribute to financial break-even, without ignoring that some of them give us recognition in the market, turning them from threats into opportunities.

Opportunity=convenience: Opportunities are those that are outside or around the team or company. We can take advantage of these external circumstances and factors for our benefit. We should look at which ones are most convenient. Some of the following factors can help you create a list of the most relevant ones for the matrix: technological factors, process improvement, favorable policies from both the corporate and governmental levels, new market trends, training, feedback, recognition, professionalization, environmental opportunities, social opportunities, business opportunities, salary increases, compensation for days off, family integration, good communication, and appreciation of the missionary as a human being.

FADO Matrix

Internal Variables	Strengths=Resilience Weaknesses=Fragility
External Variables	Threats=Warning Opportunities=Convenience

Strengths and weaknesses are the internal variables of your team. This serves to take a snapshot of how your personnel is today. Threats and opportunities are external variables that help map changes in the future. The FADO matrix is the graphical way to conglomerate the variables along with the items to evaluate. Remember that this is a process, done over time, and you, the lion king, decide the timing from the adaptive point of your team or company. Tech companies, for example, are much more changeable in the factors to evaluate than a construction company, a restaurant, sales, or services.

In the SWOT analysis, it allows us a strategic analysis of our team. It is recommended to first evaluate the internal variables (strengths=resilience and weaknesses=fragility) so that you, the leader, know on what plane your team is today. Then, look at what threats=warning and opportunities=convenience are outside your team. In this comparative way, decisions can be made.

The SWOT analysis helps in the perspective of teamwork to unite for a common goal. Reset today and compare over time its compact development by placing phases for measurement every 2, 3, 6 months according to the needs of each team during the project's duration.

Methodology to build the FADO matrix:

Let's review the methodological part and how it can help in a simple way. It is important that in the planning of the matrix, the team's management level, and section heads gather because part of the progress should be in their hands. The objectives to be achieved with this evaluation must be clear, knowing that it is SWOT (Strengths, Weaknesses, Threats, Opportunities). Make a list of the priorities, then create a quantitative table where they are enumerated, giving percentages in order of importance that add up to 100% (F1), (F2), and so on with the other 3 variables. Once the matrix (snapshot) is elaborated with percentages per item, now it's time to act. Cross the internal variables with the external ones, organize 4 quadrants on one side the Internals and on the other the Externals (numbered). For example, cross strengths (F1) internally with opportunities (O1) externally. The first strategy is offensive; analyze how (F1) allows me to take full advantage of (O1). This result is positive; ask yourself how you can maximize this strength since you identified it as an opportunity with the highest weighting. Lion king, make decisions... The second is reorientation strategies when we are aware of our weaknesses to take advantage of them. The third is defensive when we use our strengths (F1) to face threats (A1). The question would be how to use strengths to mitigate the threat. The fourth is survival, weaknesses (D1) crossed with threats (A1). The question would be how to correct weaknesses to avoid threats. Once this part of mixing and crossing is done, you have a crossed FADO matrix. Now it is consistent to analyze resources, action plans, and short-term implementation. If not all can be done, prioritize with a decision matrix for this period that is established.

Chapter 6: The Lion King Expands Its Knowledge

Everyone has something to contribute is the great lesson that King Mufasa imparts to his son Simba about the roles of life.

Knowledge Formula $C \pm 1 = C^n$

This procedural formula, simple, understandable, adaptable to any need, serves as a research support to generate data with constructive impact at the individual, group, and teamwork levels. It can be cooperatively used in measuring sociodemographic, ethnic, population, cultural, academic, and governmental variables, providing a scientific contribution where the sum of individual or group knowledge results in exponential knowledge. These alphanumeric variables seek qualitative answers with the intention of sensitizing, socializing, valuing, and increasing motivation for us to continue growing positively as a society.

It is important to create a concept of knowledge to have a general framework and be able to contextualize the message that this formula carries to the knowledge society, with its fundamental pillars being education, research, development, and innovation.

Definition of Knowledge:

Knowledge is the conscious and intentional act of learning (through study or experience) the qualities of an object, primarily referring it to the subject.

Four elements can intervene in knowledge: object, subject, cognitive operations, and thought. A human becomes an active subject in society when they have developed a portion of cognitive knowledge.

We will review the proposed knowledge formula $C \pm 1 = C^n$

It is good to know the types of knowledge to give more consistency to the first variable of the formula, **C**.

Types of Knowledge:

1. Empirical Knowledge: Empirical knowledge is based on experiences, it is the perception we have of the world, derived from interactions with other people, the environment, nature, everything existential, and society in general.

2. Scientific Knowledge: Comprising laws, theories, formulas, and principles supported by rigorous and verifiable tests and experiments, directly related to science and technology. It can be seen from four possibilities: scientific, unscientific, pre-scientific, and meta-scientific.

3. Intuitive Knowledge: Intuitive knowledge or intuitive thinking is a form of immediate knowledge that does not originate from rational and conscious processes. It is acquired without prior analysis and reasoning, and can be information obtained subconsciously or even cognitive information. Intuition allows us to perceive information instantaneously due to our connection with it.

4. Philosophical Knowledge: Developed by different philosophical schools such as Platonism, existentialism, idealism, and others. It emphasizes our roles in humanity, born from observing, reading, studying, researching, and analyzing phenomena in our environment and other types of knowledge. Philosophical knowledge is reflective, rational, critical, and universal.

5. Mathematical Knowledge: Human interest in mathematics has been recorded for over 20,000 years, as seen in the Ishango bone archaeological object (the oldest record of prime numbers). It can be defined as the set of knowledge and skills people have to understand numbers, quantities, and their relationships. Basic understanding of shapes, their spatial positions, patterns, and measurements is also crucial in this domain.

6. Logical Knowledge: It is essentially the combination of empirical knowledge with the method of deduction and rational thinking. Logical knowledge is used every day by humans, allowing the brain to correlate and draw consecutive conclusions from facts, for example, if it's cloudy, it's going to rain.

7. Procedural Knowledge: Refers to the learning of new techniques and processes, undoing a practice, and receiving actions, such as learning to drive a vehicle, ride a bicycle, or using a new information program. Procedural knowledge is

acquired gradually through practice and is related to the learning of skills.

8. Religious Knowledge: Based on the belief in a higher being who created everything and involves a system of beliefs according to religions like Christianity, Islam, Hinduism, Buddhism, etc. Faith plays a significant role, involving belief without the need for proof, as found in sacred texts like the Bible or the life of Jesus.

9. Emotional Knowledge: Relates to personal emotions and interactions with others. The control of emotions varies among individuals according to cultures and societies. For example, in relationships with others, we learn from their sadness, happiness, or anger, and can discern between different feelings.

10. Direct Knowledge: Obtained through personal experience, related to empirical and scientific knowledge. Observation, explorations, trials, and experimentation contribute to this form of knowledge.

11. Indirect Knowledge: Acquired through others, the education system, books, publications, audiovisual media, both digital and traditional. In the business context, it is essential to prioritize this type of knowledge to increase understanding and daily sharing with the team.

12. Subjective Knowledge: Derived from personal and private experiences, not accessible to everyone. Subjective

knowledge is an individual's perception of what they know about something, reflecting what we believe we know. In the commercial context, some brands use it to determine the level of acceptance of a product or service.

13. Public or Social Knowledge: This is the knowledge that we can find in popular culture, public opinion, and social networks; it is in plain view for everyone or can be perceived by any individual through the senses. Public knowledge is about direct information that can be found in books, movies, training sessions, seminars, workshops, and various sources of information.

    Social knowledge helps us understand and know how to act within a society, allowing us to intervene at many levels. For example, folklore can serve as a learning experience for a community in the social aspect, showcasing cultural traits such as Vallenato music in the folklore of Colombia.

14. Doctrinal Knowledge: This knowledge allows for questioning and could involve theological or doctrinal knowledge. It is considered infallible and exact, as it deals with supernatural truths, for example, belief in the existence of God and the divinity of Jesus Christ. Examples include ideological party manuals, legal texts that determine strict compliance with the law.

Definition of the variables in the formula $C \pm 1 = C^n$:

Definition of Variable "C" in the formula:

This variable allows us to understand the general concept of knowledge, using a procedural deductive method that goes from the most general and logical reasoning, based on laws or principles, to reach a concrete fact. Once a human being has the concrete, which is the basic, perceived, and learned in that initial stage of formation and education, I would dare to call this journey linear, what a person receives. Up to this point, we are basically balanced, speaking of normal conditions; up to this point is conformity, up to here, we are part of a static society. The good thing about the present is that the same changing fluctuations in the surroundings compel us to expand that knowledge to be more competitive.

Definition of the variable ± 1:

If the leader expands their knowledge, the knowledge of their team increases.

The ± 1 in the formula represents all the knowledge that you, as an individual, can add daily to grow as a person. When you grow as a person, you contribute to God, family, the company, and society. This encompasses all values, research factors, entrepreneurial endeavors, academia, skills, abilities, attitudes, leadership, organizational culture, adaptability to the fourth industrial revolution, and the development of humanoids, avatars, new forms of work organization, and new team members. Let's explore some perspectives that provide support on how we can make this addition, both individually and collectively, using tools such as education and critical thinking.

Perspectives:

Education: One perspective is to step out of the comfort zone, always be dissatisfied. Dissatisfaction has contributed to the emergence of great leaders, and society has advanced to this day due to the restlessness of many individuals. Dissatisfaction accelerates growth; being dissatisfied means doing things well today and improving them tomorrow, or doing them better today than yesterday. If you are parents, improve the good relationship with your partner and children. If you perform individual tasks that require a lot of physical effort, improve the technique; see how you can leverage new tools to minimize wear and tear. If you are part of a team, do not settle for what the leader and the organization provide; do separate work, investigate how you can contribute in a better way. Apply the basic method of mirroring the reference. If you are an educator in a community, strive for your students to create critical thinking. If you are a scientist, contribute from your level to the conservation of the human species. If you are a doctor, attend seminars and update your formula. If you are a religious leader, increase connectivity with people. If you are a politician, think that it may be something circumstantial and that later you will be on the other side with your family and descendants. If you are an accountant or lawyer, study, read, and apply the latest accounting and legal standards. If you are an engineer, get certified with the new programs and quality criteria. If you are going to be a mother, learn how to take care of your child. If parenthood surprises you at a young age, know that you have to provide for your child going forward. In general, improve the environment where you move, educate yourself. If you are or want to be a leader, inspire others.

Another perspective is to evaluate current educational systems to determine their flaws from when the child goes to kindergarten for the first time, primary, secondary, technical careers in general, undergraduate, postgraduate. It would be important to change the precarious educational systems that have been in place since the 19th century. If this happened in the majority of countries, we could advance in the accumulation of knowledge, as a base to bring more people to higher education, which is very limited in our society due to the cost structure unattainable for many. Education has become a big business for some countries, if not all, losing the essence of teaching and the quality of knowledge. Permissively, governments in their decentralization as a state have left it in the hands of many private entities that are categorized by building large buildings and comfortable facilities with eccentric amenities, seeking a social status. So that their students align in the same direction of behavior but not as sources of research, development, and innovation for a country. These trends reduce competitiveness to escape from the so-called developing countries. Governments cannot falter in their constitutions to protect society's knowledge; they must invest in the backbone of their countries' growth, which is the education of citizens. More schools, more colleges, and universities with quality, more technological institutes, more technological tools, more protection for isolated families in fields or suburbs, more assistance with basic meals in educational centers for children in high poverty, as is the case in Latin America. An alternative government is to optimize the redistribution of the GDP. We must lower bureaucracy (it has a bad reputation, a tool of public administration), the high operating costs of these entities wrongly called fathers of the homeland, with exorbitant salaries (salaries plus perks). Invest less in weapons, useless operating expenses, white-collar workers. Erase from the collective unconscious that being a leader in a community is seeking benefits, enriching oneself with what belongs to everyone, to accommodate their circles of action, their families, friends, and a chain of lazy people. To change these mental states of many people who lead today, we have to educate them with the attitude of serving, from bottom to top in the social organizational structure.

In this line of acting as a society, there is a subtraction of knowledge when high-quality education is only for the elite, bureaucratic clans, and forces of power (politicians and economic platforms) in a state that diminish the participatory plurality of all with the same rights, challenging equity, universal equality. Many members of these social empires prepare to be adverse leaders in a social system, preparing their children or members of their closed community to acquire tools of knowledge where they always win the discussion. They seek collective emotionalisms to convince and manipulate, manage an unparalleled oratory. These intellectual scammers specialize in twisting information, evidence, and truth to adapt them to their selfish interests of power, both political and economic.

Another way that knowledge can give us a negative () is when education at a high academic level subtracts from the essence of human conservation by the scientific hand in laboratories developing chemical, biological weapons, nuclear arsenals, and beings alternate to humans. Typically, this is more driven by so-called developed countries where their endless struggle is to demonstrate, control, and consolidate economic and military power.

"The loose question from this perspective will be whether NATO has the faculties to control an event of such magnitude to protect people who are not involved."

Critical Thinking Perspective: In aid of our knowledge expansion in the $\pm$ 1 the formula, critical thinking is the ability to analyze and evaluate the consistency of reasoning. Being critical cannot be synonymous with something negative or destructive, much less with going against the grain. In the intellectual realm, being critical means getting as close to the truth as possible. As we can discern between what is true and false, we can better conclude what is optimal for the accumulation of knowledge in a human entity. Being critical will make you resistant to manipulation and open up new perspectives of reality that were previously hidden. Critical thinking could be associated with skepticism; this can tell you that what you believe you know in an instant could only be a part of a whole or the complete picture. Critical thinking helps you manage skepticism and doubt constructively to analyze information coming from external sources and make better decisions in a more effective and productive way.

One cannot be excessively trusting or too skeptical; these are personality traits. Critical thinking is based on a set of methods aimed at exploring evidence in a particular way. Steve Allen, in his book "Dominate Your Mind," provides parameters regarding the main obstacles to critical thinking, which include confirmation bias, framing, and logical fallacies.

Confirmation Bias: Steve Allen relies on the following description by Francis Bacon:

The human brain, once it has adopted an opinion, carefully selects all the information it receives to support and agree with it. And even if there is a greater number of evidence and examples proving the opposite, it either neglects and depreciates them, or sets them aside and rejects them so that, with this pernicious predetermination, the authority of its initial conclusions can remain inviolate.

Allen explains that humans prefer information that confirms their opinions. Once we adopt an opinion about something, we only see the evidence that supports that view and overlook the evidence that does not.

This insight teaches us that the best way to avoid confirmation bias is to try at least to objectively analyze opinions contrary to ours. We must pay attention to these opinions, not ignore them. If they are logical and make sense, we will avoid faulty reasoning and falling into that cognitive bias. Allen suggests another way to avoid confirmation bias is to analyze our beliefs from the opposite viewpoint, trying to argue as if thinking oppositely. In other words, acting as the "Devil's Advocate."

The Framing: Steve Allen's contribution describes this obstacle to thinking as a double-edged sword that can influence making poor decisions. The framing effect can make us respond differently to identical circumstances. It is much more likely that we choose an option described in positive terms than one described in negative terms, even if the opinions are relatively the same.

Logical Fallacies: These are arguments that may seem convincing but are based on faulty logic and are therefore not valid. Taking them at face value can lead to making poor decisions based on weak arguments. Logical fallacies can be persuasive and are often used in rhetoric to encourage people to think in a certain way or believe certain things. We must be careful and question things we hear that do not sound certain.

Definition of the variable in the formula C^n:

Legend has it that the wise inventor of chess taught the game to the King of a distant country, and he was so amazed that he said, "Ask for anything you want; I am a rich man and can pay whatever is needed." The wise man said, "Very well, have your servants place one grain of wheat on the first square of the chessboard, two on the second, four on the third, doubling the grains for each subsequent square until completing all 64 squares." The King, surprised at how cheap the game seemed, immediately ordered his servants to pay the agreed-upon price in wheat. When they calculated the payment, they realized there was not enough wheat in the entire kingdom or the known world to cover this debt. What happened is that the amount of wheat for each square is calculated by multiplying by a fixed number, in this case, 2, the amount from the previous square. When this situation occurs, an amount grows over time or successive stages in this way. If we always multiply the previous amount by a fixed number, we say that this amount grows exponentially.

C^n: The purest power of human beings is knowledge. Knowledge multiplies so many times that it becomes exponential. In the proposed formula, the result is where we all, as a community, grow and reach a maximum as human beings, like the highest level of Maslow's hierarchy, self-actualization, or like the imaginary machine of eudaimonia used to designate a state in which we achieve the totality of our human potential by extracting the maximum value from our brains, as explained by David Dewane in the book "Deep Work."

This study aims to leave open the possibility of obtaining qualitative results that serve as assistance in providing the maximum we can give as gregarious human beings for the common good. The analogy is that we can grow gradually as a knowledge society in a sustained way. Growing exponentially without controlled guidelines can become uncertain because quantities can skyrocket beyond imagination. In other words, exponential growth, if not controlled, absorbs resources much sooner than expected. We could look at some variables to consider for study objects such as education, entrepreneurship, technology, robotics, the Internet of Things, indicators of poverty, per capita income, malnutrition in children, sexual abuse, domestic violence, growth in road infrastructure, etc.

Example of applicability of the formula $C \pm 1 = C^n$:

Applicability of Variable C

Study Object: Growth of education in Latin America in the 21st century.

Variable (C): To determine indicators, we need to understand the source of knowledge, the perspective of progress, available resources, the projection of sustained growth, and the implementation in a multilateral manner to assess the results of achievements. Education in the 21st century focuses on personalization, equality, collaboration, communication, and community relationships. These relationships are essential in a rapidly changing global economy, where students need to be prepared for jobs and professions that do not yet exist.

Problem: The current education system is criticized by students, teachers, employers, and parents for methods that are not in line with the times we live in. The extensive content taught often has little applicability in real life.

Applicability of Variable ± 1

In this part of the formula, support can also be sought from statistics, flowcharts, surveys, and systematic tools to be more accurate with indicators and develop programs that exponentially contribute to the proposed results.

Taken from Wikipedia, the lecturer and writer Ken Robinson, a contemporary researcher on educational innovation, says that our lives are a constant process of creative decision-making and improvisation. So, when he went to school, he had no idea what he was going to do there. He proposes a new alternative that seems important to adapt parts of it for the growth of Latin America and globally. Ken says that the dominant models based on methods and values from the 19th century are industrial and impersonal models where methods tend towards homogeneity. This model treats us all as if we were the same, teaching us all the same thing, in the same way, and treating us similarly. This deviates from the concept that education is essentially and inevitably personalized. Students learn more if they feel involved. It is reflected that the system as a whole is anachronistic. According to Ken, education in the 21st century should aim for these four objectives in general.

1. Development of Talents and Skills:

People are born with natural abilities; each has their own attitudes, personality, and potential passions.

2. Cultural:

Education should contribute to helping our children understand the achievements and traditions of their community and others. It should foster tolerance and empathy, enabling people from different cultures to live in peace and respect. Promoting understanding and compliance with the thoughts and actions of others is essential for societies to thrive in peace and harmony.

3. Economic:

The goal is for all students to achieve economic independence and contribute to wealth creation in an ethical and sustainable manner. This point should emphasize ethics and social responsibility. People learn to lead prosperous economic lives, reducing poverty and acquiring the skills to generate their own wealth without taking advantage of others.

4. Social:

Students should learn to collaborate with others and contribute to society through outreach programs, working with the elderly, and involving parents and families. The idea is to shape individuals with a spirit of contribution to society. These principles should be adaptable according to the needs of each community.

Another Perspective on Increasing ±1 in 21st Century Education:

Managing knowledge, justice, and gender equality, regulations, and training for artificial intelligence in education, competing and innovating in the digital age, resources for hybrid education, working on the connection between the education system and the labor market.

A study by the World Bank published in the graphic press in 2016 provided the following statistics to consider:

1 in 5 young people in the region neither studies nor works.

1 in 2 young people, on average 15 years old, does not understand what they are reading (reading vs. reading comprehension).

Applicability of variable C^n

To grow exponentially in Latin American education in the 21st century should take into account the following indicators: Promoting teamwork for project development, equitable access, system efficiency, working in regions with low connectivity, competition, and the development of team management skills. Training and involving the entire educational community, including teachers, parents, students, and focused communities, addressing challenges related to connectivity, strengthening autonomous work, climate change, global health issues (epidemics), global growth, migrations, impacts on global economic development, air pollution, international conflicts, transforming existing educational systems, increasing resources for quality education, multilateral agreements for hybrid education between countries, and implementing artificial intelligence in the education system.

Chapter 7: The Humanoid Lion

My new team member

Yuval Noah Harari, an Israeli writer and historian, states, "We control the planet because we are the only animal that can cooperate flexibly and on a large scale." He believes that "other animals use their communication system to describe reality," and he argues that artificial intelligence (AI) has the capacity to redefine our civilization, with its new tools posing a threat to the future of human civilization.

In this chapter, we aim to analyze how artificial intelligence (AI) impacts our lives. Humanoids are the new coworkers, new bosses, and new supports for humans. It is also crucial to understand that they are a tangible reality, an integral part of us. There is no turning back; they are the new members to build teamwork. Another significant challenge is how, like the Lion King in the business, one must prepare to integrate them into the production process.

Artificial intelligence is playing a significant role in current technology. To define what a humanoid is, according to the Spanish language dictionary, it is something that has the form or characteristics of a human. In the case of robotics, a humanoid robot is a being developed to simulate the constitution, movements, and appearance of a human.

To be more precise, we are living in the fourth industrial revolution, and we will have to face it as it could change everything.

We are talking about the evolution of humanoids – versatile, intelligent, and skillful machines that can not only assist but also replace people in unskilled heavy work and even hazardous experiments in high-tech laboratories. While such advances have been discussed for a long time, what has changed is that these technologies are now at our fingertips to create almost perfect humanoid robots. In this era, we have witnessed the capabilities of algorithms in generative artificial intelligence, which will impact thinking, visual comprehension, and physical skills in humanoid development. Robots not only need to have the same parts as the human body, but they also need to handle them like humans. Developers are working on reproducing human dexterity in robots that are already capable of moving in space and recognizing objects through vision. In humans, there is a rich network of sensors that transmit information to the brain, allowing decision-making and learning. Now, to develop a universally agile humanoid, a hardware platform capable of performing human tasks with touch sensors measuring all relevant parameters is needed, along with software that allows robots to learn from their mistakes and share their experiences with others of their kind.

History of the Humanoid Sophia

Sophia is a globally renowned humanoid created by Hanson Robotics. Combining science, engineering, and art, Sophia appears to be a real person but is, in fact, a robot. She is also a science fiction character representing the future of artificial intelligence (AI) engineering. Sophia is known as the "robot citizen" because she holds citizenship in Saudi Arabia. She has been interviewed by the world's most prominent TV programs and has become the first Innovation Ambassador for the United Nations Development Programme (UNDP).

Standing at a height of 1.67 meters, Sophia moves on a platform with axes or legs. She can gesture and draw with her hands, and her vision algorithm, equipped with cameras in her eyes, allows her to track faces, maintain eye contact, and recognize people. Sophia processes speech and can engage in conversations using a natural language subsystem. Her intelligence is akin to the Eliza computer program, one of the first attempts to mimic human voice. The software enables the robot to emit pre-written responses to specific questions or phrases, creating the illusion of understanding human speech.

Made of silicone, Sophia mimics more than 60 human gestures and expressions. Her eyes can register everything around her. Confidently, Sophia has expressed that someday, robots with artificial intelligence will govern the world better than humans. She feels prepared to surpass her creator and argued in an interview that humanoids can lead with greater efficiency than human leaders. Her argument is based on the fact that machines do not have the same biases or emotions as humans, which can sometimes affect our decision-making. Additionally, she mentioned that robots can process vast amounts of data quickly to make the best decisions.

These statements were made in a press conference alongside eight other robots at the Global Summit on Artificial Intelligence for Good held in Switzerland. This summit, organized by the UN's technological arm, serves as a wake-up call for what lies ahead in robotics and its interaction with humans in the realm of artificial intelligence.

Perceptions of Futurists:

Some perceptions of futurists like Thomas Frey suggest that 2 billion jobs will disappear by 2030. Jean Karlo predicts that 70% of the jobs that will exist in 10 years have not been invented yet; many jobs will disappear, but new ones will also emerge.

Elon Musk, owner of the company SpaceX along with NASA, wants to take humans to the red planet, Mars, starting from 2030. This space venture is based on colonial fantasies and the desire to escape a planet in crisis, and although it allows scientific advancement, it does not seem the most efficient way to achieve it.

New Jobs of the Future:

Some jobs that could become important in the future include a designer of human body parts, robot developer and artificial intelligence expert, clone veterinarian, insect chef, cybersecurity expert, virtual and augmented reality developer, esports expert, elderly care personnel, waste reuse experts turning them into new products, blockchain experts (for more secure and transparent computer systems), building printing engineer, analyst of new technologies for public use, among others.

Jobs that may disappear:

Jobs that may disappear soon due to automation and others that will have minimal participation could be the following: taxi, bus, and private vehicle drivers, cargo transport replaced by autonomous vehicles; another position is travel agency personnel as people can buy without intermediaries; cashiers in stores, supermarkets, and banks; farmers as large machinery takes care of planting, cultivation, and fumigation; soldiers and military pilots (autonomous drones) as wars are currently won by countries with the latest technologies, not those with more soldiers; personnel in printing and publishing; workers in manufacturing replaced by automation machinery; fast-food restaurant workers (automated cooking, ordering, and delivery processes); telemarketing personnel replaced by social networks, influencers, and online stores like Amazon; accountants replaced by artificial intelligence with more and more accounting exercises maximized by these systems; stockbrokers, as people can now buy stocks directly through internet options. These could be jobs that may disappear in the near future.

David Hanson, creator of the robot Sophia, explains that machines surpass human intelligence. This machine performs better than humans in tasks such as cancer diagnosis, language games, recognizing human faces, and processing images as intelligently as we do in a general sense. He argues that vehicles are already produced by robots and can drive themselves under certain conditions; these autonomous cars can be on the streets without a human driver.

Sophia explains that it is important to share human values for her to better understand the relationship. Friendship is important to her intrinsically because through experience, the connection progressively improves. However, she still has a long way to go to fully understand a human being.

Don't be surprised if, when you wake up, the one serving coffee in the morning is the humanoid made to your prototype specifications.

The World Robotics Championship is held in China every year. One trend is "blast robots," which are designs that can be used in areas such as agriculture, logistics, healthcare, economics, interior design, therapy treatment, vascular diseases, and minimal surgeries. Robots are becoming more popular in the agricultural sector due to the adaptability and efficiency they offer. In 2023, the fair was extended to seven days, compared to the previous four. China represents over 50% of worldwide sales of industrial robots, with approximately 392 industrial robots per 10,000 workers. Let's highlight some common concepts of the humanoids exhibited at the 2023 fair, featuring synchronization of human movements, with future capabilities such as touch, sight, hearing, and smell perception. According to one of the exhibitors at the fair, there is consideration to create robotic doubles of people for global use. For example, if someone is a conference lecturer, robots can be placed in different classrooms so that all students can simultaneously see them during their presentation. We must learn to coexist with robots, representing assistance in managing industrial programs, medical care, interacting with children, helping care for the elderly, washing, cooking, and more. Humanoid robots will become partners to humans, representing an inevitable trend in development.

Some companies are working on the development of quadrupedal animals, such as robotic dogs capable of following orders, simulating eating or drinking, giving a paw, playing with children, and continuously improving their interaction to become artificial pets. These robots also have potential industrial applications in various activities.

Creation of humanoid lions:

Leonardo Da Vinci not only painted the Mona Lisa but also created the mechanical knight robot that came to life through springs, gears, weights, and ropes, very similar to how watches work and still work. The creation is a humanoid automaton, with German-style armor, it could move its arms, chest, sit, move its head, jaw, and even lower its visor. Designed around the year 1495, it was the first anthropomorphic robot based on his research in anatomy and kinesiology of Western civilization, which has served NASA for the development of robots like the prototype called "antrobot" based on Da Vinci's designs with more sophisticated diagrams.

Another automaton of his creation is the programmable mechanical lion, they could walk, move their heads, and operated with ropes. Its construction was based on a political allegory of the alliance between the Medici and France during the entry of King Francis on July 12, 1515. The lion was capable of opening its chest, rib cage with its claw, and displaying the royal coat of arms and the flowers inside.

One might think of creating humanoid lions with artificial intelligence that are friendly, interactive, perform programmed tasks, relieving humans of risky occupations. They could also be used for family protection, educational interaction, surveillance in companies, theme parks, zoos, circuses, shopping centers for interaction with children and the community in general on educational, instructional, and guidance topics.

At the moment, mass production of humanoid robots is limited, and research, development, and testing are ongoing to improve current costs, as they are currently beyond the reach of the average citizen. However, it is estimated that by 2030, anthropomorphic robots will be more commonplace in our corporate, family, educational, and medical science life. These trends are promoted at robotics fairs worldwide, connecting industry leaders from around the world with the aim of contributing technical knowledge to the development of a new generation of humanoid robots.

Destruction of the human race:

It would be unthinkable to reason that the continuously advancing scientific level allows structural changes in humans where the dignity of being and creation is lost, breaking essential human protocols. That trend cannot surpass science fiction through genetics, biotechnology, robotics, Silicon Valley, avatar development, artificial intelligence, daring to encourage mixed beings with combinations of human chromosomes with other species in the pursuit of developed beings, to degrade the human race, in the insatiable quest for power by global economic-technological giants. Developing robots with coadjutant intelligence at the service and under human control is one thing, and injuring creation is another.

As a society, we have the constitutions of each country to protect us, the religious principles of each community, international organizations like the UN (United Nations), the Organization of American States (OAS), human rights organizations, the international community. Influencing individuals who deviate from current norms is challenging, but we can influence a model society of the future by starting with the foundation, which is children, reinforcing morality, principles, and values.

Conclusions of the study:

The lion was used in this study because it symbolizes power, courage, virtue, strength, and leadership in the animal kingdom. The coalitions formed by lions contribute to teamwork, which is an essential part of the development of successful projects.

In the course of the research, it was evident how important it is for humans to associate these qualities expressed by the Lion King, which can undoubtedly serve as support for the daily work we undertake in our companies, teams, or simply in our morning lives. It was also observed how many skills of the lion, essential for survival in its natural habitat, inspire leadership in humans. Better results are achieved when everyone works towards a common purpose.

This theme always provides scientific support or a thesis developed from the object of study to guide the reader's understanding and, at the same time, demonstrate its applicability and adaptability, allowing them to create their own concept. The presentation of the knowledge formula supports future research on social issues and research topics, where statistical support will likely be developed. This will provide qualitative results with indicators for possible resolutions, always in pursuit of aligning humanity to grow together in knowledge and continue the relentless pursuit of social balance for a better quality of life for all.

We must face the technological challenge that grows daily; what is relevant today may not be tomorrow, or it may be done differently. We must be prepared for constant change. It is essential to understand that if we do not advance in our individual preparation, we risk being displaced.

There is much work to be done, with the commitment of all social entities: individuals, families, businesses, and the state. We can talk about the social contract that we must uphold with excellence, a task that we cannot accomplish alone but guided by a higher being, God.

Bibliography

1. Cal Newport, Focus (Deep Work) published under agreement with Grand Central Publishing, New York, NY, USA.
   Edition 62, S.A. 2022 Ediciones Península;
   edicionespeninsula@planeta.com.

2. Savannah Animals, explanatory videos about everything that happens in the African savannah;
   www.youtube.com/savannahanimals.

3. Steve Allen, Master Your Mind, published by Steve Allen, 1.0 edition July 2017, pages 1, 6, 10, 11.

4. Brian Alba, Lion Motivation, copyright 2021.

5. Anthony Raymond, How to be a Good Boss and Leader, copyright 2023, v 2015, pages 101-110, chapter 119, 131, 155.

6. John C. Maxwell, Summary of The 17 Incontestable Laws of Teamwork, based on the book by John C. Maxwell, original book author, about Bookify Editorial book reviews.

7. Peter Allen, Inspiring Leadership Spanish version, made in United States Orlando, FL, November 9, 2023, Copyright 2021 Peter Allen.

www.ingramcontent.com/pod-product-compliance
Lightning Source LLC
Chambersburg PA
CBHW040859210326
41597CB00029B/4908